FAMILY CELEBRATIONS AT BIRTHDAYS

Also by Ann Hibbard

Family Celebrations at Easter
Family Celebrations at Christmas
Family Celebrations at Thanksgiving: And Alternatives to Halloween

FAMILY CELEBRATIONS AT BIRTHDAYS

And for Vacations and Other Holidays

Ann Hibbard

A Raven's Ridge Book

 Baker Books

A Division of Baker Book House Co
Grand Rapids, Michigan 49516

Published by Raven's Ridge Books
an imprint of Baker Book House Company
P.O. Box 6287, Grand Rapids, MI 49516-6287

Printed in the United States of America

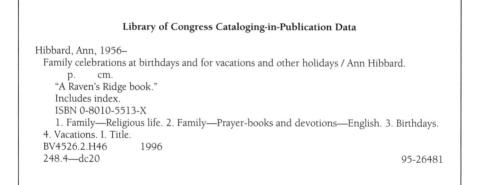

Library of Congress Cataloging-in-Publication Data

Hibbard, Ann, 1956–
    Family celebrations at birthdays and for vacations and other holidays / Ann Hibbard.
        p.   cm.
    "A Raven's Ridge book."
    Includes index.
    ISBN 0-8010-5513-X
    1. Family—Religious life. 2. Family—Prayer-books and devotions—English. 3. Birthdays.
4. Vacations. I. Title.
BV4526.2.H46   1996
248.4—dc20   95-26481

"The Road to Calvary" originally appeared in *Family Celebrations: Meeting Christ in Your Holidays and Special Occasions* by Ann Hibbard.

Contents

A NOTE TO PARENTS

H ere is the final book in the series of Family Celebrations books published by Baker Book House. It is perhaps the most eclectic of the four books, covering birthdays, family vacations, Valentine's Day, Mother's Day, Father's Day, and, as a special bonus, "The Road to Calvary" devotions and corresponding banner for Lent.

Except for the bonus section, this book focuses on "lesser holidays." These are not "holy days" in the celebration of the church year, yet they are important times in the life of the family. And as Christian families, we want to invite Christ to hold the place of preeminence on these occasions as well as at Christmas and Easter.

In this book more than the others, I have shared advice on how to celebrate these holidays. Because my experience is limited to my childhood memories and now my own family's practices, I interviewed a number of other Christian women, ranging in age from early thirties to seventies. Some are referred to by name, others by pseudonym, and others, though also helping me to shape my thoughts on these family celebrations, are not given individual mention.

Specifically, I would like to thank Beth Adams, Barbara Andrukonis, Debbie Bennetch, Anne Cregger, Louise Knudsen, Sheridan Larson, Evelyn Oltman, Louise Pearson, Beth Spring, Virginia Watson, and Susan Yates. I also want to thank my "coaches," Steve Griffith and Steve Rigell.

Of course, my family plays a prominent role in how I view family celebrations. I owe a tremendous debt of gratitude to my parents, Marilynn Martin and Lester Martin, and to my two sisters, Carolyn Bizien and Elaine Nesbit. Last but not least (or as Laura once said, "least but not last"), hats off to my terrific family—Laura, Mark, and Jim. Thanks for letting me share our stories.

AVOIDING THE BIRTHDAY TRAPS

I f you are one of those mothers who absolutely loves throwing parties for your children, who looks forward to your children's birthdays with eagerness, this chapter is not for you. Skip ahead to the next one.

I confess it. I am not one of those wonderful mothers. My children's birthday cakes will never grace the cover of *Family Circle* magazine. No one talks about and imitates our children's birthday parties.

Some people thrive on organizing fun parties for their children; unfortunately, I am not one of them. I have a very low tolerance for noise and confusion. This particular disability qualifies me as "birthday party challenged."

So why am I writing about celebrating birthdays? Good question. The fact of the matter is that parents who handle their children's birthdays with ease don't need a book. We who struggle need the advice and guidance. And advice from superorganized, on-top-of-things moms just doesn't help us very much.

Despite our limitations, we love our children tremendously, and we want to make their birthdays special. Certainly we don't want to disappoint them. On this day more than any other we want them to know how precious they are to us.

Yet birthdays often seem like minefields. Everywhere we turn there are problems, and we seldom anticipate them.

The "Inflated Expectations" Trap

"Next year for my birthday party, I want to . . ." Laura began. I could hardly believe my ears. I paused and looked up at my eight-year-old daughter, who had just said good-bye to the last guest at her birthday party. I was literally scraping the cake off the plates and into the garbage. The girl hadn't even digested this year's birthday cake, and she was already formulating plans for next year!

Many children think about their birthdays for the entire year. By the time the big day rolls around, they fully expect a genie to shoot out of a magic lamp, Aladdin-style, and grant them three wishes. They envision shooting stars and swirling colors. They long to be hoisted on the shoulders of family and friends and paraded through the streets amid cheers and thundering applause.

Is it any wonder many parents dread their children's birthdays? Who could live up to such a vision? Inflated expectations plague many families at birthday time. No birthday party could possibly fulfill such fantasies. How does a parent keep from disappointing this imaginative and hopeful child?

One way is to *talk about expectations ahead of time.* Find out what your child expects the birthday to be like. If his or her vision is not grounded in reality, you may need to issue some gentle warnings. Lovingly help your child to adjust his or her expectations.

Also, you should *plan the birthday wisely.* By all means, allow the child some say in how his or her birthday is celebrated. But remember, you are older and wiser. You can foresee that some scenarios will work better than others. If you exercise that guidance, you may prevent fully avoidable situations that would cause pain or disappointment on your child's birthday.

The "Selfishness Syndrome" Trap

The "selfishness syndrome" trap is closely tied to the "inflated expectations" trap. The birthday child who is honored as King for a Day suddenly turns into a little tyrant. He expects everyone to wait on him hand and foot. Doing chores is out of the question in the child's mind. After all, it's his *birthday!*

As they say, "Power corrupts, and absolute power corrupts absolutely." Children cannot handle carte blanche—on their birthday or any other day. So don't give it to them. *Explain that while it is their special day, when they will enjoy certain special privileges, they are still members of a family.* As such, they are required to participate in certain chores. They can choose the menu for dinner, but they must still obey their parents and be kind to their siblings.

The "Overstimulation" Trap

Virginia and Frank have a son whose birthday, like my Laura's, falls right around Easter. For his fourth birthday, they came up with what they thought would be a surefire success—an Easter egg hunt. They knocked themselves out filling plastic eggs with goodies and hiding them around their yard. A dozen or so preschoolers arrived decked out and ready for a good time.

When it came time for the Easter egg hunt, only a few of the children caught on to the idea. They began racing around collecting plastic eggs. Most of the children, however, were overwhelmed by the task. As they saw the others getting all the eggs, they sent up a howl.

Frank and Virginia found themselves surrounded by frustrated four-year-olds bawling their heads off. They ran here and there trying to comfort, calm, and assist the host of upset children. What had promised to be a fun event turned into a disaster.

From this incident, Virginia learned some important lessons. She learned *not to invite so many children*. A good rule of thumb is to have the same number of children as the age of the birthday child. She also learned to *keep the activities simple and age appropriate*.

Both of these guidelines help prevent a birthday party from getting out of control. When things are out of control, children become confused, hyperactive, and easily upset—not exactly the formula for a fun birthday party.

Nor will it be a fun birthday party if the birthday child feels overwhelmed. My friend Anne has a son who dreads his own birthday because he has a hard time handling all the attention. Parents need to *be aware of their children's emotional reactions*. Some personalities recoil when the spotlight shines on them. A child like this prefers a low-key birthday—a fun time that does not require him or her to be in the limelight.

The "Bigger and Better Birthday" Trap

A huge charter bus rolled into the parking lot of the Christian school. When the principal asked what was happening, the bus driver explained that he was there to pick up all the seventh-grade boys.

"I didn't know that we had a field trip planned," the principal remarked. "No, sir. This is a birthday party," came the bus driver's reply. Just then a familiar BMW swerved into the parking lot, and out jumped the mother of one of the seventh-grade boys. She explained the plans to the awestruck principal: The bus would take the boys to the football stadium where that city's professional football team played. She had hired a number of the pro football players to play football with her son and all of his school friends for his birthday. Not only that, the entire squad of cheerleaders would be there to cheer them on—skimpy outfits and all.

One teenage girl's parents hired a chauffeur to drive her and two of her friends in a stretch limousine from their home in Washington, D.C., to New York City for a rock concert. The chauffeur waited in the parking lot for the girls, then drove them home in the wee hours of the morning.

Try topping those birthday parties. I wonder what the boys and girls who attended those events expected for their next birthday celebrations.

The subtle pressure to compete with other parents in the birthday department is something that I call the "bigger and better birthday" trap. My friend Susan tells me that in some communities, particularly in the South, this pressure is very real. The amount of money you spend on your child's birthday party determines how wonderful (or mediocre) a parent you are.

Our own children can also perpetuate this trap. They go to a murder mystery birthday party and decide that they want the same kind of party—only scarier and more elaborate.

My advice to those who struggle with this pressure: Determine not to buy into it. Stay off the bandwagon. Take the risk of being thought weird, impoverished, boring, or neglectful.

Use your imagination rather than your pocketbook. The children will appreciate a simple, well-planned party if the activities are creative and the atmosphere is one of warmth and love. Our friends the Adamses hosted a mystery party for their daughter Rachel. The girls at the party were given the mission of finding the "lost princess." They found clues hidden at various locations throughout the house that eventually led them to the lost princess. This was big sister Katie dressed in full princess regalia (thrift shop acquisitions). Neither expensive nor elaborate, this party ranks top on my daughter Laura's list of favorite birthday parties. All it took was a little time and imagination.

Explore alternatives to children's birthday parties. Instead of the typical children's party, plan a special family outing in honor of your child's birthday. Go to the circus, the Ice Capades, an NBA basketball game or other sports event, or the rodeo. Take the family bowling or miniature golfing and out to an ice-cream parlor afterwards. The possibilities are endless.

Ultimately, many find that family outings on birthdays are more satisfying than children's parties.

The "Too Many Presents" Trap

When Sandy and her husband, Chris, committed their lives to Christ, they adopted a lifestyle that leaves Sandy's folks baffled and at times intimidated. These lifestyle differences clash especially at holidays and birthdays. Sandy's parents delight in giving their grandchildren lots of gifts on their birthdays. They spare no expense. Sandy and Chris don't want their children to have so many toys. They don't like the clutter, and they especially don't like what it does to their children's attitudes. Greed and materialism crowd out gratitude and hunger for God.

After discussing it together, Sandy and Chris went to Sandy's parents with a proposal: "We appreciate so much the way your love overflows in generosity on our kids' birthdays," they began. "You are terrific grandparents. The kids love you so much—you know that.

"We have been having some trouble with the kids over their gifts, and we wanted to let you know about it. Right now they have so many toys that they really don't seem to value them very much. It seems like all we do is yell at them to pick up their toys so they won't get lost or broken. We are wondering how you would feel about getting each child one nice gift for his or her birthday? For instance, Scott could really use a new bike for his birthday next month."

Sandy's parents responded well to their respectful appeal. One Christmas they even gave all the children a nice computer system, which has been a great educational tool for the entire family. Sandy and Chris knew they could not ask her parents not to spend so much money on their children. That was how her parents showed their love. Rather, Sandy and Chris came up with a compromise, which they presented in a spirit of humility and love.

Often children themselves fall into the "too many presents" trap. They want to invite lots of children to their party because they want to receive lots of "loot." If you detect this attitude in your child, do him or her a favor and nip it in the bud. *Limit the number of children* invited to the party. Your child will probably enjoy a special activity with one to three other children just as much as a huge party with lots of children—and this automatically limits how many gifts your child will receive.

Limit the amount that people spend on the gifts by specifying the limit on the invitation ("Please limit your gift to something under $10"). Another option is to have a party with no gifts (funny cards only).

Don't neglect thank-you notes, written by your child to all those who gave gifts. This takes an enormous amount of prodding. It's not fun, for you or for your child, but it is essential training in consideration and gratitude. Plus, once your child catches on to the fact that each gift will require a personally written, thoughtful thank-you note, he or she may not be so eager to accumulate a mountain of gifts.

The "Jealous Sibling" Trap

Sibling rivalry has been around since Cain and Abel. It is a normal, though exasperating, part of family life. Birthdays often heighten this rivalry. In one family with two sons, one son disappeared during his brother's birthday party. The parents found him several hours later, hiding in a dark closet. The little boy just couldn't bear watching his brother receive so much attention and acclaim, not to mention gifts!

One way to avoid the "jealous sibling" trap is to *talk about possible feelings of jealousy* prior to a birthday in a way that children can understand. I love the children's book *A Birthday for Frances* by Russell Hoban. In it, Frances the badger struggles with jealousy on the day of her little sister Gloria's birthday. She finds it especially hard to give Gloria her delicious birthday present, a "Chompo" bar. Frances reveals her true feelings as she sings her version of the birthday song in which she expresses the desire to have the Chompo bar for herself.

If this is a problem in your home, I recommend purchasing this book and reading it as a family prior to your children's birthdays. We can all relate to Frances, and her hilarious expressions of jealousy help us to identify these feelings within ourselves.

Frances comes around in the end, providing the reader with a wonderful lesson in love and generosity. When jealousy or sibling rivalry crop up in real life, you can use Frances as a point of reference, in a way that is funny, not preachy.

Another way to avoid the "jealous sibling" trap is to *involve the sibling in the joy of giving*. If the sibling has chosen or made a birthday gift and has helped to wrap it, that child will look forward to seeing the birthday child open the gift. Now that our children are older and have some outside income, we expect them to pay for gifts for family members. This contributes to their sense of involvement. And the result is that they look forward to giving gifts as much as they do receiving them.

(Note: Be sure to coach the birthday child in showing enthusiasm and appreciation for the gifts as he or she opens them. Our practice is to hug family members and thank them immediately.)

Gifts That Really Matter

Birthdays, like other holidays, tend to bring out either the best or the worst in us. And sometimes they bring out both! Beneath these birthday traps lie issues like guilt, pride, selfishness, and laziness—on the part of the parents as well as the children.

Too many parents these days have little time or energy for their children. In an effort to assuage their guilt, they spend money on their children. This excessive spending reaches tremendous heights at Christmas and on birthdays. But the children are not fooled. They know deep down that love cannot be bought and sold. Elaborate, expensive birthday parties are no substitute for a parent's loving presence, day in and day out.

Just as important, we need to teach our children that we do not show love for a person by spending money on him or her. Love is shown in little acts of kindness and thoughtfulness. A word of praise, a sweet note in a lunch box, a warm hug on a bad day—these are the things that demonstrate love.

Our children desperately need our love. Not presents and privileges. Just love. Children know that they are loved when we give them the *gift of our time*. Mrs. Oltman, our family friend and piano teacher, relates that countless children sit at her piano and tell her,

"My parents don't have time for me." Those parents probably have no clue that their children feel that way. Unintentionally the parents have communicated this message to their children by their busyness and overinvolvement in outside activities.

We demonstrate our love for our children when we give them the *gift of honor*. My parents were masters at this. They always praised me. When their friends said nice things about me, they always told me. Never once did I doubt my parents' love for me. I had the unshakable conviction that they believed in me, and that knowledge has stood me in good stead every day of my life.

Birthdays are opportunities for us to give our children the gift of honor, but it doesn't work if we do this only once a year. The birthday should be the climax of an entire year of showing honor. If the child feels loved and honored all year long, he or she can handle the privileges of the birthday with a bit more equilibrium.

One specific way that we can recognize our child on his or her birthday, and on other special days, is to fly a birthday flag in his or her honor. A birthday flag bears the name of the child in huge letters and emblems signifying activities and achievements that have been important to the child. (Complete instructions for making a birthday flag appear in the resources section.)

When this flag waves in the breeze outside your home, everyone knows that it is that child's special day. You can even put the flag out when your child arrives home from camp—or college. Some children may not like so much fanfare, but most of us appreciate a public salute once in a while!

Perhaps most important, we need to give our children the *gift of grace*. That means meeting their failures with forgiveness and restoration. It means accepting them no matter what they do or say. It means loving them when they are at their most unlovable.

It's easy to love our children when they snuggle up to us or when they lie fast asleep looking like angels. Love doesn't come as easily when your two-year-old throws himself down in the parking lot in a full-blown temper tantrum. Or when your teenage daughter screams "I hate you!" and runs to her room, slamming the door after her (yes, it will happen to you too).

These are the moments when we need to remember another birthday—the birthday of our Lord Jesus Christ. He came to earth in order to experience our humanity. He understands our feelings of helplessness and frustration, and the rage that comes of caring so deeply. He knows what it is to love those who cannot see beyond themselves.

But the primary reason Christ came to earth was to give his life for us, so that we could experience his grace. His death has provided innumerable blessings to us, who deserve only his wrath. Because of his birth (and death), he extends to us the second birth, as God's adopted children. And that is the beginning of a life undergirded with the loving care of the heavenly Father and propelled toward an eternity with him.

As we endeavor to become wise and loving parents, and as we negotiate birthdays and other challenges, let us remember God's gift of grace to us. If we extend this grace to our children, we give them a gift that all the birthdays in the world cannot begin to match.

MOMS HAVE BIRTHDAYS TOO

I t had been a difficult year. At age thirty-nine, Karen had given birth to her fourth boy. Now he was five months old, and Karen was turning forty. It seemed like a big milestone, but nothing seemed to be brewing for her birthday. Karen didn't detect any sidelong glances or secretive outings. Nothing.

Finally, the afternoon of her birthday, the kids were in a frenzy. Karen overheard them talking to their father on the phone. "Dad, it's Mom's birthday, and we don't have anything! What are we going to do?" Karen knew without hearing it what her husband, Bob, was saying: "Don't worry. I'll stop on the way home from work and pick up something."

Bob arrived home with a package under his arm and immediately rushed upstairs with the kids. Soon they all reappeared with two hastily wrapped presents.

The plan was to open presents first, then Bob would take Karen out to dinner. They did this every year for Karen's birthday.

As Karen opened her gifts, she smiled and thanked the boys, but beneath her pleasant demeanor, the pressure was rising. She and Bob said good-bye to the boys and hopped in the car.

Apparently she hadn't done a perfect job of concealing her feelings, for Bob turned to Karen and asked, "What's the matter with you?"

"You want to know what's the matter with me?" Karen exploded. "I'll tell you what's the matter with me. This is my fortieth birthday. I have a five-month-old baby at home, and you're stopping at the drugstore on the way home from work to get me perfume and earrings for my birthday present. Forget it! I'd rather you forgot the whole thing!"

Barely pausing for breath, she continued, "It hurts my feelings that as horrible a year as this has been for me, I'm not more of a priority for you. I'm not looking for riches! I'm looking for value! I want to know that you think I'm special. And this celebration didn't do it, Bob."

This situation is all too familiar in homes across North America. Yet many of us lack Karen's honesty and courage to deal directly with our disappointment. Instead, we silently fume and let bitterness burrow its roots into our spirit. Or else we convince ourselves that our birthday didn't matter that much anyway. After all, we're grown-ups, right? And by the time we're forty, birthdays shouldn't be such a big deal.

But the fact of the matter is, they are. A birthday is the one day of the year set aside to honor a person, not for anything she has accomplished, but simply for being who she is. And that's important!

Often, however, our birthdays leave us disappointed and depressed. Several problems are evident in Karen's situation that are common to many less-than-perfect adult birthdays.

The Problem of Preparation

Let's face it, children do not naturally think, "Oh, my goodness, in two weeks it's Mom's birthday! What kind of party would really make her happy? And what has she been looking at longingly in the sales flyers?" It just doesn't happen!

And even when they do remember, until they are of driving age, children are fairly helpless to do anything about it. They can't get to the store to buy presents or decorations.

In families where there is a mom and a dad, the ball is in Dad's court. It's up to Dad to rally the children to plan and prepare for Mom's special day. Yet many husbands have as much enthusiasm for planning a fantasy birthday as they do for going to the dentist. They act like they're allergic to stores, and they avoid them at all costs.

In homes without a dad, other family members and close friends can step in to fill the void. Several years ago, I hosted a birthday party for a single friend and her three children. If I had really been thinking, I would have whisked the children off prior to Kathy's birthday and taken them shopping for her present. Most friends would be happy to do this, but we don't because it simply doesn't occur to us.

If you are a single mom, don't hesitate to ask a friend to take your children shopping for your gift. You're not doing it for yourself. This will relieve your children of a great burden of anxiety and guilt.

The Problem of Presents

It's the classic scenario. We give the gift that we would really like to receive. The wife gives her husband a stylish shirt and sweater ensemble. Although he appreciates it, the gift doesn't thrill him. The husband is excited to give his wife a nifty computer program to help her manage the family finances. Needless to say, that was not what she was hoping to find beneath the wrapping paper.

Author and speaker Dee Brestin tells of one husband who couldn't wait to have his wife unwrap her gift. He knew that she would love this item because she had been complaining for so long that the old one was broken. The wife tore off the paper and there was a toilet seat!

My friend Sandy recounted that she told her husband, "The day you give me a salad spinner for my birthday, it's all over!" Another couple I know has dealt with this problem by agreeing not to exchange birthday gifts.

Why Bother?

When it seems like so much effort, you can't help but ask yourself, "Why bother?" Here's why: *Thoughtfulness abounds in loving homes.* Love isn't love unless it is demonstrated, and being thoughtful of our family members is how we make our love evident. If we want our homes to be loving (and who doesn't?), we need to work together to establish patterns of thoughtfulness.

Birthdays are made-to-order opportunities for showing family members that we think they are special—and that we value them. Birthdays only come once a year, so it is not expecting too much that the family put a little bit of thought, time, and preparation into making the mother or the father feel honored that day.

We also need to work at showing thoughtfulness to family members on their birthdays because *we are training future husbands and wives.* My friend Anne was disappointed recently in the lack of preparation her sons put into her birthday. The following day, she confronted them.

"Guys, this wasn't good," she said. "You need to do better than this—not for me, but just in general, in terms of honoring the mother or the father in the house. You need to give it more thought and action. When you're adults, this will mean a lot to your wives."

In order for our children to grow up to be good husbands and wives, they need to understand the importance of thoughtfulness. And thoughtfulness takes some planning and some effort.

What does a lack of thoughtfulness say? It says, "I was too busy with my own important activities to be thinking about your birthday."

Thoughtfulness teaches unselfishness. Teaching our children to remember our birthdays and those of others is a good way to reinforce that the world does not revolve around them.

Yet trying to teach our children to be thoughtful is like trying to teach them respect. It's difficult to insist on it. The best way to teach children thoughtfulness is by example.

The rest of this chapter contains some tips that might help.

Perform Acts of Thoughtfulness

I call my friend Martha "the Birthday Queen." No one is more diligent about remembering birthdays than Martha. And I speak with good authority. Martha lived with our family for three years, so I observed firsthand how she faithfully remembered a seemingly infinite number of birthdays—friends, family members, and former roommates (a total of thirty-six before she moved in with us).

Believe me, Martha single-handedly keeps Hallmark in business!

Martha's thoughtfulness was contagious. Before long, I felt uncomfortable with my hit-or-miss approach to the birthdays of friends and relatives. I learned from Martha that it is simply a matter of recording people's birthdays on my calendar, then transferring them to the next year's calendar at the end of the year. It doesn't take long to pick up a card when one is out running errands. I just needed to be a bit more organized and intentional. Often Martha picked out all the cards for that month in one stop at the card shop.

That little extra effort goes a long way. It feels good to be on the receiving end of Martha's thoughtfulness. When September 17 approaches, I know that Martha is thinking of me and will make an effort to get together with me, or at least send me a card.

Just as Martha's acts of thoughtfulness rubbed off on me, *our example cannot help but influence our children.* If our children see us remembering others' birthdays on a regular basis, chances are they will grow up to do the same. Thoughtfulness will not seem like a huge effort. It will be "standard operating procedure."

Examine Expectations

As we move from childhood into adulthood, we bring with us ideas of how life should be. Because birthdays are a very important part of childhood, our memories (good or bad) of childhood birthday celebrations shape our expectations of our adult birthdays.

Then we marry someone with a completely different set of experiences, hence a different set of expectations.

This is where problems often arise. Mary grew up in a rather well-to-do family where huge, elaborate parties and lavish gifts were how her parents showed their love. Her husband, Bill, came from a family of humbler means and a simpler lifestyle, where they celebrated birthdays with a small but meaningful family dinner. The presents were not expensive, but they were carefully chosen.

Mary kept waiting for Bill to plan a wonderful surprise party in her honor, but year after year, her hopes were dashed. Bill couldn't figure out why the gifts he painstakingly selected for her failed to satisfy. And so the cycle continued, disappointment turning to resentment, driving an icy wedge between them.

If we want to break this destructive cycle, *we need to take a good, hard look at our expectations.* We must ask ourselves, "Are these expectations justified?" Just because our family of origin celebrated birthdays one way doesn't mean that it is the only way to celebrate birthdays.

It is my opinion that we have a right to expect our spouse to remember our birthday and plan some way to celebrate the day in our honor. But what shape that celebration takes will be unique to the spouse. We need to recognize the fact that our spouse did not grow up in the same family that we did.

Then we must ask ourselves, "Are these expectations realistic?" Bill is brilliant in technical areas. He keeps current on state-of-the-art computer programs and hardware. He has no interest, however, in following the fashion industry. For him to select a stylish, well-made garment for Mary's birthday simply lies outside the realm of possibility. Mary has learned that if she wants to get an article of clothing for her birthday, it helps him if she specifies exactly what she desires. (The catalog number, if possible!)

Because Bill is so good with technical things, Mary has begun to request such gifts for her birthday. Then she feels free to go out and buy the clothes that she needs for herself.

My friend Anne has had several huge surprise birthday parties in recent years orchestrated by her husband. Brian even secretly arranged to fly in her best friend from high school whom she had not seen in years. For most wives to expect such a celebration would be unfair to their husbands. Party planning does not come naturally to many men.

Realistic expectations take into account the strengths and weaknesses of our partner. They allow for mitigating circumstances. When the family budget is stretched to the limit, it isn't realistic to expect our spouse to spend hundreds of dollars on a birthday gift. A simpler birthday is more appropriate.

As children observe thoughtfulness and realistic expectations demonstrated by their parents toward each other, they too will internalize these important qualities and will be better prepared to be thoughtful, loving husbands and wives.

Communicate Well in Advance

Once we have dealt with our expectations, *we need to let our loved ones know how we would like to celebrate our birthday.* We can't expect them to read our mind.

It helps if this is done with a good measure of humor. My friend Virginia relates how her husband, Frank, prepares everyone for his birthday each year.

Sometime in June, he'll begin to make remarks like, "Did you know that Sonny Jergensen and Gene Kelly will be celebrating their birthdays soon?"

The listener will invariably respond, "Sonny Jergensen and Gene Kelly? When is that?" "Well, it's the twenty-third of August," says Frank. "How did you know that?" Frank's audience asks. Without a moment's hesitation, Frank replies, "Well, another famous American's birthday is the twenty-third of August."

This kind of tongue-in-cheek advertising does more than help people remember our birthday. It adds a heaping tablespoon of fun to the birthday recipe. And people love to participate in things that are fun—much more so than if it is seen as a "duty."

Beyond reminding people that our birthday is approaching, we need to communicate clearly our desires for that day. Last September I wanted to make my son Mark's birthday a special one, but he couldn't decide what he wanted as a gift. Nearly every day I bugged him about it. Every suggestion I made he nixed.

Finally his birthday arrived and he still had not made up his mind. I made him a delicious birthday dinner (at least he figured out what he wanted to eat!), and we honored him at a family celebration. But there were no presents at all. The relatives had sent money (which he wanted), and his sister, Laura, had given him her gift early. I struggled not to feel guilty, but what could I do?

A week or so later, Mark came up with an idea for a birthday gift. I bought it, wrapped it up, and tucked it in with all of my presents on the night of my birthday celebration. Mark was surprised and thrilled when one of the gifts was for him—and it was just what he wanted.

If we don't tell people what we want, we can't expect them to do it for us.

Form a Birthday Club

Every year I try to talk my mom into coming to visit us in April so that she can celebrate her birthday with us. I figure, Mom's single, which means she doesn't have a husband to take her out for her birthday. Surely she would want to come and be with us so she doesn't feel lonely. Wrong. No way does Mom want to miss her birthday in Minneapolis.

You see, Mom belongs to two birthday clubs, which are groups of friends that celebrate each member's birthday. One of these groups consists of eight women who take turns hosting luncheons for each others' birthdays. The other consists of three couples plus Mom—all longtime friends. This group celebrates with a dessert gathering in honor of the birthday person. Additionally, Mom has several close girlfriends who take her out on her birthday. (And of course my sister Elaine, who lives in the area, always puts on a fabulous family celebration for Mom.)

Despite the fact that two of her three daughters live far away, Mom always has plenty going that last week of April. I too have been blessed with a number of wonderful friends who always remember my birthday and do something to make it special for me. And of course I do the same for them. *Celebrating with friends* is not only deeply satisfying for adults, it takes pressure off our family to meet all our "birthday needs," and provides our children with another example of thoughtfulness.

Remember Your Mother on Your Birthday

Since I've become a mother, I've realized that the birthday is just as important to the mother as it is to the birthday child (whether that child is a youngster or an adult).

This certainly is true for my mother. If at all possible, Mom tries to be here for my birthday; she wants to be with me for the celebration. On the years that she cannot come, she calls first thing in the morning to wish me a happy birthday. She always recounts the details of my birth. It was a tremendously important day for her— one of the most significant days of her entire life, she says.

My friend Anne shared with me a wonderful idea. She and her siblings have a tradition in which they give their mother a small gift on their own birthdays. It is a way of saying, "Thank you for giving life to me." *We should remember to honor our mothers on the day that holds such special significance for them.*

Practice Gracious Gift-Receiving

Frank really knows how to help his family enjoy celebrating his birthday. Virginia tells me that Frank sets the standard for good gift receivers: "No matter what you give him, he opens up the present and oohs and aahs about it. You may have completely missed the mark. Yet even if he never looks at it again, he says, 'Oh, this is interesting! Where did you find it?'"

Of course, this response is very rewarding to the giver. The family has often made a big deal of Frank's birthdays as a result. More importantly, however, Frank has set for his family a good example of appreciating the gift because the giver gave it.

He doesn't ask himself, "Is this what I wanted?" Nor does he expect the present to show how much he is worth to the giver. *He simply appreciates the thought, time, and effort that went into the giving of the gift.*

And that's really the bottom line, isn't it? A gift is, after all, a gift. It is not a payment nor is it the fulfilling of an obligation.

In the spiritual realm, we recognize that we are the recipients of God's gifts. Our salvation is a free gift from God. We did nothing to deserve it. All we do is humbly accept it. In fact, all the blessings in our lives come from God, the giver of all good gifts.

Birthdays are a wonderful opportunity to play out that spiritual reality. In establishing patterns of generous, warmhearted giving and receiving in our homes, we reenact God's goodness to us. We freely and cheerfully give to others in love, mirroring God's abundant grace. And as we accept gifts with humble, grateful spirits, we show our children and the world a picture of what it means to be God's beloved child.

FAMILY DEVOTIONS
FOR BIRTHDAYS

BIRTHDAY 1

One of my favorite children's books is *Rasmus and the Vagabond* by Astrid Lindgren. Rasmus was a dark-eyed little boy with freckles spattered across his face who lived in an orphanage in Sweden. Every day Rasmus had to hoe potatoes and pull nettles under the stern eye of Miss Hawk, the woman who ran the orphanage. More than anything else, Rasmus wanted to be adopted by one of the nice couples who came to the orphanage. But they always seemed to choose the polite girls with blond, curly hair.

If you have ever been the last one picked for a team—or worse yet, not picked at all, you know just how Rasmus felt. Finally, in frustration, Rasmus ran away from the orphanage. He would try on his own to find a home. What he found instead was a kind tramp named Paradise Oscar. After many exciting adventures, Oscar led him to a new home where he would be loved completely.

Do you know someone who is adopted? Perhaps you are. If so, that is especially wonderful because of what it shows us about God's love. The Bible tells us that all who love him are adopted by God.

Read—*Ephesians 1:4–6*

For he chose us in him before the creation of the world to be holy and blameless in his sight. In love he predestined us to be adopted as his sons through Jesus Christ, in accordance with his pleasure and will—to the praise of his glorious grace, which he has freely given us in the One he loves.

Discuss

1. When did God choose us?
2. Predestined means decided ahead of time. What did God decide ahead of time for us? Why?
3. What did God have in mind for us?

4. When you think about God choosing you before he even created the world, how does that make you feel?

Final Thought

These amazing truths should make us, like Paul, want to praise God for his goodness. It is because of Jesus' death on the cross that we can receive all these good things from God and can be adopted as his children. It doesn't really matter if we have blond curls and are smart and pretty. What matters is whether we belong to the one who loves us completely.

Pray

Heavenly Father, we know that we belong to you not because of our goodness, but because of your goodness and grace. Help us always to remember who we are, and that we belong to you. In Jesus' name. Amen.

Sing—*The King of Love My Shepherd Is* (p. 201)

The King of love my shepherd is,
Whose goodness faileth never;
I nothing lack if I am his,
And he is mine forever.

And so, through all the length of days,
Thy goodness faileth never.
Good Shepherd, may I sing thy praise
Within thy house forever.

Do

Tell what being God's child means to you (have everyone share).

Are there some things about your-self that you would change if you could? Perhaps it is your nose, or your ears, or your hair. Perhaps you would make yourself smarter or more athletic.

I didn't worry too much about how I looked until I was in seventh grade. Of course, that was when the pimples appeared. "If only I didn't have zits," I would moan to my reflection in the mirror. But there they were, as plain as day. Although I treated them and covered them up as best I could, they still did not go away. I knew that I would never be a beauty queen, so I decided to be good at other things. I worked hard to get good grades in school, and I tried to be a kind, nice person. When people talked to me, I smiled and looked them straight in the eye. I wanted them to see my eyes and my smile and hear my words, rather than noticing my pimples. God gave me pimples for a good reason. They helped me to develop my inner self.

Read—*Psalm 139:13–16*

For you created my inmost being;
   you knit me together in my mother's womb.
I praise you because I am fearfully and wonderfully made;
   your works are wonderful, I know that full well.
My frame was not hidden from you
   when I was made in the secret place.
When I was woven together in the depths of the earth,
   your eyes saw my unformed body.
All the days ordained for me
   were written in your book before one of them came to be.

Discuss

1. What do these verses tell us about how we were made?
2. How do these verses show that we are important to God?
3. Why do you think we mean so much to God?

4. Verse 16 says that all our days are written in God's book. That means that our whole life is important to God, and every single day counts to him. How does it make you feel when you think about this?

Final Thought

The next time you wish that you looked like someone else, or you had someone else's brains or abilities, remember that God fashioned you just as carefully as he did that other person. He had a reason for every feature, every ability that he gave you. He made you perfectly. That is, perfectly *you*—made to order by the greatest designer ever—God.

Pray

Dear Lord, thank you that you designed each of us the way you did for your special purposes. Help us to remember how important we are to you and to love you all our days. In Jesus' name. Amen.

Sing—*The King of Love My Shepherd Is* (p. 201)

The King of love my shepherd is,
Whose goodness faileth never;
I nothing lack if I am his,
And he is mine forever.

And so, through all the length of days,
Thy goodness faileth never.
Good Shepherd, may I sing thy praise
Within thy house forever.

Do

Write out Psalm 139:14 and tape it to your mirror.

BIRTHDAY 3

In our home, our children must do many chores. When they complain that they feel like slaves, I remind them of all that a mother does so that they don't feel like they are alone in their slave labor! As hard as we may work, we are far from being slaves. Slaves were people who, because they were captured or poor, were sold to rich people. They couldn't go where they wanted to go or do what they wanted to do. They had to do exactly what their master said.

Imagine what it would be like to be born to a slave family. As a young boy or girl, you could be sold by your master to someone else. You would be separated from your parents, and could never be with them again. And what if your new master was cruel? What if he beat you? This happened to many slave children.

The Bible tells us that everyone born into this world is a slave—and the master is sin. That means that we are not free to do what is right and to love and know God. We have to do what our master, sin, tells us to do.

God doesn't want us to be slaves. But in order for us to be set free, we need to be bought from our master, sin. Someone needs to pay the price for us. The following verses tell us who already paid for us, and the price that was paid for our freedom.

Read—*1 Peter 1:18–19*

For you know that it was not with perishable things such as silver or gold that you were redeemed from the empty way of life handed down to you from your forefathers, but with the precious blood of Christ, a lamb without blemish or defect.

Discuss

1. To redeem someone means to free that person from something bad by paying a price. Who paid for us to be set free?
2. What did he pay?

3. Which is more precious to God, gold and silver, or his son?
4. If God paid such a high price for you, what does that tell you about how important you are to him?

Final Thought

What do you think is the most valuable thing in the world? The world's largest diamond perhaps? Yet there is nothing about a diamond that makes it more valuable than an ordinary rock. What makes it valuable is the amount of money that people are willing to spend on it. In the same way, what makes us valuable is the price that God was willing to pay for us.

Pray

Dear Lord, thank you for paying the highest price ever—your own life and blood—to buy us away from sin. Thank you that we are valuable to you. Thank you that we are free to love and obey you, instead of having to mind the cruel master, sin. Help us to live our lives like free people, not like slaves to sin. In Jesus' name. Amen.

Sing—*Savior, like a Shepherd Lead Us* (p. 206)

Savior, like a shepherd lead us;
Much we need your tender care.
In your pleasant pastures feed us,
For our use your fold prepare.
Blessed Jesus, blessed Jesus,
You have bought us; we are yours.

Do

Act out the redemption of a slave and talk about how that relates to Jesus redeeming us.

Do you sometimes feel that you just don't have what it takes? Perhaps you've been given a job that seems too hard for you. All you can think about is what you're not good at doing. "I'll never amount to anything!" you think in disgust.

Everyone feels that way sometimes. God doesn't want us to feel that way, though. In his Word, he tells us that we are all special to him. He has a special plan for each of us if we are willing to obey him.

One day God spoke to a man named Jeremiah. God had a hard job for him. He wanted Jeremiah to be his prophet, to give his message to the people of Israel. Read God's words to Jeremiah and see if they teach you anything about God's plan for you.

Read—*Jeremiah 1:4–10*

The word of the LORD came to me, saying,

> "Before I formed you in the womb I knew you,
>   before you were born I set you apart;
>   I appointed you as a prophet to the nations."

"Ah, Sovereign LORD," I said, "I do not know how to speak; I am only a child."

But the LORD said to me, "Do not say, 'I am only a child.' You must go to everyone I send you to and say whatever I command you. Do not be afraid of them, for I am with you and will rescue you," declares the LORD.

Then the LORD reached out his hand and touched my mouth and said to me, "Now, I have put my words in your mouth. See, today I appoint you over nations and kingdoms to uproot and tear down, to destroy and overthrow, to build and to plant."

Discuss

1. When did God first know Jeremiah? When did he decide that Jeremiah would be his prophet?

2. What did Jeremiah say? How was he feeling?
3. What did God say and do to give Jeremiah the confidence that he needed?
4. How can you know what God wants you to do and be? What should you remember if you are afraid?

Final Thought

God probably won't call you to be a prophet like Jeremiah—thank goodness! But how will you know what he is calling you to do? Here's how to find out: Simply love him and do what you already know he wants you to do. Then when he calls you to a special job, you'll be in a place where you can hear his voice.

Pray

Father, today we thank you especially for _____ (the name of the birthday child) and the special person that you have created him (her) to be. You have a plan for his (her) life, Lord. Help him (her) to remember this, and to remember that you will always be with him (her). Amen.

Sing—*Take My Life, that I May Be* (pp. 188–89)

Take my life, that I may be
Consecrated, Lord, to thee;
Take my moments and my days;
Let them flow in ceaseless praise.

Take my love; my Lord, I pour
At thy feet its treasure store;
Take myself, and I will be
Ever, only, all for thee.

Do

Have each member of the family name one thing about the birthday child that is special or that he or she especially appreciates.

MAKING THE MOST
OF FAMILY VACATIONS

Everyone had raved about family vacations on North Carolina's Outer Banks, how it was the perfect place to relax with small children. Not for us, I thought bitterly after battling frustration and stress for the better part of a week.

Three-year-old Mark was terrified of everything. Instead of happily playing in the sand, Mark perched on top of two upside-down plastic pails to avoid the skittering sand crabs. The waves sent him into hysterics. Jim and I finally gave up trying to introduce Mark to the ocean.

Laura, on the other hand, immediately fell in love with the ocean. If I didn't watch over her like a hawk, our toddler would plunge into the frigid waters and give herself over to the undertow.

I tried to walk along the beach with the children, but it wasn't easy. Mark held my hand on the land side, pulling me away from the water. With the other hand I firmly grasped Laura as she pulled me toward the ocean. Whenever she could, she broke free and tumbled into the surf, emerging with a gleam in her eye and an ear-to-ear grin. Meanwhile, I felt as if I were being drawn and quartered!

As parents, we want family vacations to be perfectly wonderful, stressfree, fun family times. We want to create happy memories for our children. We want to have fun as a family. Additionally, we want a break from our own routines—either to kick up our feet and relax or to see new sights and enjoy different experiences.

This is a tall order for a one- or two-week period. Too tall, in fact. Realistically, most families find that vacationing together adds stress rather than alleviating it. Why? For one thing, change is stressful. When we deviate from our usual routine, our schedules are upset and we find ourselves faced with all sorts of decisions that we normally do not have to make. The most basic of functions, such as where and when to eat supper, require deliberation.

Then our differences rub against one another and produce friction. Our two children's opposite reactions to the ocean presented us with a parental dilemma. Should we go to the beach, where Laura will be happy but Mark will be miserable? Or should we stay in the cottage, where Mark can be content playing with Legos? Or should we each take one child and spend the entire vacation apart?

Often the most stressful differences surface in the marriage relationship. Last summer my friend Liz and her family traveled from

Virginia to the southwestern United States. Liz is a planner. She had spent months planning every detail of the trip. Efficient and cost conscious, she had each day programmed to maximize the family's experiences, to take in all that the American Southwest has to offer.

They arrived at their hotel in a quaint Arizona town, and the first thing her husband, Ron, did was switch on the TV—in the middle of the day.

"What do you think you're doing?" Liz demanded.

"This is my vacation. I'm relaxing," Ron replied, removing his shoes. "Besides, I've got to see how our baseball team is doing."

"Ron, we are in a historic western town. We're only going to be here for one day, and we'll never be back here again. I want to see it before we move on to the Grand Canyon," Liz insisted, thinking of the thousands of dollars they were spending on this vacation.

Liz's and Ron's conflicting expectations came to a head on this vacation. They were forced to deal with the fact that they have very different personalities, different vacationing styles, and different needs. Ron needed "veg-out" time to recuperate from the grind of a demanding full-time job. Liz, usually cloistered at home with young children, needed to see new vistas and to experience mental stimulation.

What is the solution? Should we throw up our hands and give up on family vacations? Some people do. I have heard of couples who deal with their differences by taking separate vacations.

Those who take this route miss out on some of the best opportunities for growth that family life has to offer. Family vacations can work. I can attest to this. Our family made changes in our vacations since that infamous week at the Outer Banks—and the changes have made for deeply satisfying family times. Best of all, our children regard our vacations as the high point of the year. They treasure those times together as a family. And we are a stronger, more loving family as a result of our experiences during our annual getaway.

What changes can we make in order to transform our family vacations from times of disagreement and frustration to times of cooperation and delight? A commitment to communicate, compromise, and seek new challenges is a good start.

Communicate

Faced with marriage-straining differences on their Southwest vacation, Liz and Ron realized that they needed to communicate better—before the vacation. No more Lone Ranger planning for Liz. She needed to pull Ron into the planning process. Now when they begin to formulate plans for a vacation, they discuss their individual needs, desires, and expectations.

As our children grow older, they too should have a voice in determining the shape of the family vacations. Several years ago, we were camping in the mountains when a hurricane-spawned weather system headed our way. As rain pelted down on our tent and threatened to seep through the bottom corners, Jim and I discussed packing up and retreating to our dry, snug home.

"Are you talking about going back home?" Laura piped up.

"We're thinking of it," I answered.

Laura's brow furrowed, and she said indignantly, "When you're camping, you don't just give up! You survive!"

Laura saved our vacation. We did survive the rain and went on to enjoy a week of glorious weather and fabulous hiking.

Sometimes we forget the obvious—that our loved ones are distinct individuals whose desires differ from ours. Vacations are important to them too, and we need to take into account which aspects they value most. The only way we can find out how they feel and what they want is to ask—and then listen.

Communication is only the beginning, however. If we solicit someone's opinion, then proceed to do exactly what we want to do despite their opinion, we will find our family in serious trouble. Essentially our actions say, "I'm only pretending to care how you feel and what you want. You're not really important here. I'm the only one who counts."

Compromise

In loving relationships, after communication the next step is compromise. Somehow we need to accommodate our differing needs and desires. Compromise requires that everyone give a little.

And giving is what being a family is all about, isn't it? Jesus set the standard for love when he laid down his own life for us. He commands us to demonstrate the same kind of love to one another—self-sacrificing love.

That sounds very sweet and nice. In theory we agree, but when it comes to things like planning how we will spend our vacations, we all want to have our own way. Selfishness rears its ugly head.

Let's begin to look at vacations as opportunities to love our families by laying down our lives in small ways. As we compromise, adjust, and accommodate, we may find that it's not so painful after all. And the resulting blessings make the sacrifice more than worthwhile.

Beach vacations having been less than successful, now our family spends our vacations hiking in the mountains. All of us enjoy this. If we happen to camp near a lake, we often take an afternoon or two off from our usual hiking regimen so that Laura, still our water baby, can get in some beach time. This involves sacrifice for Jim and Mark, but they do it because they love Laura and going to the beach is important to her. Compromise.

Challenge

Finally, I have found that a secret to fun and memorable family vacations lies in challenging oneself.

"Ugh! That sounds awful!" you may think. "I face enough challenges in my normal daily routine. When it's time to vacation, I don't want to think—I don't want to do—I just want to relax."

Perhaps. But often what we think we need and what we really need are two completely different things.

Last spring I served as chaperone on Laura's class overnight retreat to Camp Hemlock. The focus of the retreat was the ropes course, where groups of ten students were given difficult tasks to accomplish or obstacles to overcome. They had to solve these problems by working cooperatively and without help from adults.

At first these kids had no interest in group problem solving. All they wanted to do was fool around. But the counselor firmly yet positively directed the students to the task. A total transformation occurred before my eyes that day: I saw an unruly bunch of sixth graders become a team. I watched them as they learned to listen to each person and value each opinion. I saw a formerly shy boy emerge as a true (and excellent) leader. And we all had a blast!

What was the secret? Challenge and direction. As the children met challenge after challenge and overcame obstacles, their confidence grew. It was exhilarating to discover that they could do things they never thought they could do. And they were able to do these "impossible" things because they were given direction in how to work together as a group. The structure that they so resisted actually enabled them to enjoy themselves. As it turned out, they had much more fun doing the ropes course than they had had at other events where they were given free rein.

The same principles hold true with families. Challenges, when faced together, force us to depend on each other, to work together, and to grow, both individually and as a family unit. The structure of God's law sets boundaries on our behavior. We respond to each other in loving ways that build each other up and make for a positive experience. Growing together is lots of fun!

Last summer as we hiked up a mountain in Maine's Acadia National Park, our family reminisced about all our camping trips over the past ten years.

"Remember that long hike in the highlands of Cape Breton, Nova Scotia?"

"Yeah! Can you believe that we made it all day on only one canteen of water for the whole family?"

"Well, don't forget, we did eat lots of blueberries. They kept us from getting dehydrated."

Our fondest memories are of times we conquered some seemingly insurmountable obstacle, learned new things, or met interesting people. Through communicating with each other, compromising, and challenging ourselves to grow, we have found the secret of enriching family vacations.

FOCUS ON GROWTH

S o you want to make a change in your family vacations. You want these times to be satisfying, enriching times of growth. Where do you begin—short of signing up for Outward Bound? Growth takes place in many different areas of our lives. Let's take a look at some specific ideas for stimulating growth on family vacations in four areas—physical, mental, relational, and spiritual.

Physical Growth

Camping presents many opportunities for physical challenge. Without all of our modern conveniences, we discover what life was like for most of humankind throughout the ages—and how much of their time and energy was devoted to meeting physical needs. Fortunately for us, this is something we do for fun, not out of necessity.

Beginning when he was tiny, Mark accompanied Jim on his forays into the woods to collect fallen branches for firewood. The two of them would emerge from the forest dragging long branches behind them. Mark couldn't conceal a look of pride and delight in his accomplishment. Then as soon as he was able, Mark learned how to saw and chop wood. After working up a sweat chopping firewood, Mark's voice dropped an octave. Obviously he felt like a man. I watched amazed as Mark's sense of identity grew through taking on these physical challenges.

Last summer in Maine the entire family faced a new physical challenge. We had hiked up the spine of Dorr Mountain to its highest point. There we discovered a different trail down, the Precipice. Everyone warned us, "If you're going to hike the Precipice, hike it up the mountain, not down." But we were already up. We needed to get down, and the rest of my family was game for the challenge.

Then we saw the sign that read,

THE PRECIPICE IS MAINTAINED AS A NONTECHNICAL CLIMBING ROUTE, NOT A HIKING TRAIL. ATTEMPT THIS ROUTE ONLY IF YOU ARE PHYSICALLY FIT, WEARING BOOTS, AND EXPERIENCED IN EXPOSURE TO HEIGHTS. PERSONS HAVE FALLEN AND DIED ON THIS MOUNTAINSIDE.

"That does it," I said. "I'm not going down that trail. Absolutely not. I refuse." My family prevailed, and before long I found myself grasping iron handholds and inching along ledges in the sheer rock face.

Although I didn't thrive on the feeling of danger and the threat of sure and sudden death, the rest of my family loved it. That hike topped their list of favorites. Why? Because of the challenge, the pure fun of conquering a formidable obstacle.

Brainstorm together about physical challenges that would be appropriate and fun for your family. Even tiny children enjoy canoeing or going out in a paddleboat. As they get older, family biking becomes a possibility. Or perhaps your family prefers skiing or tennis. By the time your children are teenagers, the sky is the limit. They are ready for rappelling, scuba diving, and bungee jumping!

Mental Growth

In his poem "Happy Thought," Robert Louis Stevenson wrote, "The world is so full of a number of things that we should all be as happy as kings." Discovery brings joy. If we approach life with an attitude of anticipation, always seeking to learn new things, we will be happier people. And this is just as true on family vacations as it is in day-to-day life.

Going on ranger-led hikes is one of our favorite activities when camping. We have found the rangers in our national parks to be not only knowledgeable in their fields, but also gifted communicators.

Last summer in Acadia, a ranger taught us how to survive on a particular mountain should we get lost or stranded. We learned how to make a pot for boiling water out of birch bark, which plants and berries were edible, and how to treat a headache or a cough. She also taught us things about nature, such as how to distinguish a fir tree from a spruce tree.

After spending time learning from rangers, our eyes were open to these aspects of nature. Our new awareness made hiking more enjoyable. We were no longer hiking simply "to get to the top," but we were noticing the wonders of God's creation along the way.

There are many ways to challenge yourself mentally on family vacations. Before you leave home, find some fiction books set in the area you will be visiting. If you will be traveling to Maine, for instance, go to the library and check out *Miss Rumphius* by Barbara

Cooney, and *Blueberries for Sal* and *One Morning in Maine* by Robert McCloskey. Read these excellent children's books as a family. This will heighten everyone's anticipation and enrich your visit once you reach your destination.

Do your family members have interests in plant life, earth science, or birds? Go to the library and check out a guidebook on trees of the area you are visiting. When your family goes hiking, bring the guidebook along and try to identify trees by examining their leaves, bark, and other characteristics. If you are spending a week at the ocean, find a book that explains tides in simple terms. Then learn by experience. Mark the high tide. When the tide is low, measure the distance between high and low tide. If your family likes bird watching, take along a field guide and some binoculars. Keep a record of all the birds you spot.

Is someone in your family of an artistic bent? Bring along a sketch pad and pencils for drawing, or a notebook for writing poetry. Be sure to allow your artist quiet time for creating—and give him or her lots of praise for his or her endeavors.

I always keep a journal of our family vacations. In it I record our activities, where we stayed, where we bought groceries, and so forth. This helps if we ever return to that area or if we recommend it to friends. More important, I write down the funny things the kids said and did and the interesting things we experienced together. These journal entries preserve memories that cannot be captured in photographs.

Every place has a history, and it is fun to learn about what life was like in days gone by. If you are visiting a well-known historical site, check out books appropriate for the ages of your children and read aloud interesting, pertinent information about the events that took place there. Last summer, when visiting family in Idaho, I spent time in the authentic old gold-mining town of Idaho City. We even panned for gold in a creek.

I'll never forget the time when our children were very young and we toured the Biltmore House in Asheville, North Carolina. This incredible mansion is filled with priceless pieces of art and furniture from all over the world. When we entered one bedroom, there stood the most breathtaking canopy bed we had ever seen. Laura, age six, took one look at it and said, "Mom, *that's* the bed I've been wanting!"

It is also interesting to explore the industry of the locale you are visiting. Ask what people do there to earn a living. Often plants give free tours of their facilities. We have toured coal mines, auto manufacturing plants, and naval vessels. After several trips to Maine, we have learned quite a bit about the lobster industry there. Check out the local library or visitor's information center for ideas.

Relational Growth

Vacations provide opportunities for growth in relationships, whether you are visiting relatives or friends or you are vacationing alone with your own family.

If you are visiting relatives, investigate your roots. Older folks love to pass on stories of their childhood and young adulthood. When you show interest in their past, they feel valued. As an added bonus, you will hear interesting stories and glean new insights into the lives and personalities of loved ones.

Recently when my mom was visiting us, she told us about her first job. As a high school student, she worked part time in the hospital in her rural community. We listened enthralled as she recounted her experience of spending the night alone in the hospital, the lone "professional" in charge of all the patients. She gave injections, strapped down patients who were "climbing the walls," and called the doctor when someone was dying. (The doctor simply told her to call the mortuary once the patient was dead!) How things have changed since then!

Find out about your relatives' childhoods, what they did for fun, who their friends were, what chores they did, what school was like for them. As you discover new things about loved ones, you will be enriched with a sense of your own history and identity, and your relationships with them will deepen.

What about your own family? Vacations often strain these fundamental relationships. How can you turn these times around into opportunities for family growth?

Determine to work as a team on your family vacation. Each person in the family should feel like a valued member of the team. That means that everyone treats everyone else with respect. (For instance, tell your children that they will be expected to treat each other as they want to be treated. Have them provide specific examples.)

Be sure to explain this rule of behavior clearly at the outset. If it has not recently been the *modus operandi* in your home, you can expect your children to test you. Stand firm. It's a good investment. Setting high standards for how you treat each other may be difficult at first, but it pays great dividends.

Vacations are no break for Mom if she is expected to do all the work, without the conveniences of home. Take the team approach and share the workload. After ten years of family camping, we have it down to a science. From setting up camp to preparing and cleaning up meals to doing laundry to breaking camp, we work together. Each person has a job to do, and our routine works like clockwork. This approach goes a long way toward eliminating stress because there is no arguing about who does what.

As you work together cooperatively, encouraging each other, you will find that you also play together better. Your times of relaxation and recreation will be sweeter, and they will reflect the team spirit that you have worked to develop.

Spiritual Growth

Many people "check out" spiritually when they go on vacation. Some do it intentionally, figuring that they need a break from that routine as well. I wish I were a good enough person that I didn't *need* to spend time daily with the Lord. But I desperately need those moments alone with Christ each day. I need his forgiveness, his wisdom, his guidance—whether I am at home or on the road.

Most of us struggle with maintaining a regular quiet time when we are on vacation. We are not in our regular routine. Often we do not control our schedule. Everything seems to conspire to keep us from spending time with God.

Yet vacations can be times of spiritual growth, both as individuals and as families. The first step is to pray that the Lord will make it so. He understands that we battle against the world, the flesh, and the devil. We are not able to win that war in our own strength. Just as in the days of Joshua, he wants it known that "the battle is the Lord's."

He will provide everything that we need to grow in him, if we just present to him our need and depend on him to fulfill it.

The second step is to make Christ a priority on our vacation. That may mean waking up a half hour earlier. Or it may mean excusing yourself from the hubbub of relatives in order to find a quiet spot to pray and read the Scriptures. The Lord will not force you to do this. He wants you to exercise your will. That is a very real part of loving him.

The third step is to invite Christ into the moment-by-moment activities of the vacation. As we encounter difficulties, we can turn to him in prayer. Then we can rejoice together as we watch God answer our prayers.

My friend Louise and her family spent many vacations camping all across Europe, where her husband was stationed in the navy. With three children and little money, they sometimes found themselves utterly dependent on the Lord for the most basic necessities. Yet these strained times provided great opportunity for spiritual growth as a family.

One memorable vacation their family faced rain, rain, and more rain as they camped in Germany. Each day as they approached their destination, they prayed that God would stop the rain long enough for them to pitch their two pup tents. Sure enough, just as they rolled into the campground, the rain stopped. No sooner would they get the tents up than the rain would begin again. They experienced God's faithfulness, and their faith grew.

The fourth step is to take time as a family to look into God's Word—daily. It can be in the morning around the breakfast table, or at night in front of a blazing campfire. No matter where or when, just do it. You will be surprised at the difference it will make in your vacation if your family spends just a few minutes each day reflecting on God's Word, acknowledging his Lordship, and committing the family's ways to him.

God's Word is amazingly relevant to the situations we encounter on vacation. One night we camped in one of the highest campgrounds along the Blue Ridge Parkway. As we set up, we noticed gray mist swirling around us. We were actually in the clouds. During supper a thunderstorm hit. Lightning seemed to be crashing all around us. It was a new and frightening experience to be in the heart of a thunderstorm.

The next morning, storm over, we managed to get a fire started despite our waterlogged firewood. As we huddled around the smoking fire, we turned to our devotions (the same devotions that follow in this book). We had been looking each day at Moses and the Israelites in the wilderness. This day's devotion happened to be on Moses' meeting with God on top of Mount Sinai, where God caused a violent thunderstorm. Our understanding of that passage had moved from the theoretical to the real. We knew just how Moses felt!

On another occasion, we were hiking along a ridge trail and, not being experienced hikers at the time, we had not brought any water along. Mark, age seven, was struggling to make it on the return hike. But, significantly, he was not complaining. Finally, he rounded a bend and saw a drinking fountain that marked the end of the trail. He burst out, "Mom, the Lord made it be the end of the trail. I knew I shouldn't complain like the Israelites did, so I prayed and God helped me to make it!" I silently praised God to see that my son's faith was growing as he learned to apply God's Word to his life.

So this year as you vacation, prepare to grow—physically, mentally, relationally, and spiritually. May God bless you with an enriching time as a family. But even more important, may you come to know his faithfulness as you learn to depend on him.

FAMILY DEVOTIONS FOR VACATION

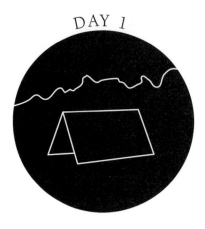

DAY 1

Why is your family taking a vacation? One reason is to take a break from work and the regular routine, to have some relaxing family time. Long ago, God's people, the Israelites, went on a very long trip. They desperately needed a break—a big one! The Israelites were slaves in Egypt. Their masters were cruel to them and beat them. God heard their cries and their prayers and answered them. He chose Moses to lead them. About two million Israelites started out on that long trip in the middle of the night. Can you imagine what it was like, all those people getting ready to leave? The worst of it was, they didn't even know where they were going or how to get there!

They just knew that God told them to leave.

Read—*Exodus 13:17–18, 20–22*

When Pharaoh let the people go, God did not lead them on the road through the Philistine country, though that was shorter. For God said, "If they face war, they might change their minds and return to Egypt." So God led the people around by the desert road toward the Red Sea. The Israelites went up out of Egypt armed for battle. . . .

After leaving Succoth they camped at Etham on the edge of the desert. By day the LORD went ahead of them in a pillar of cloud to guide them on their way and by night in a pillar of fire to give them light, so that they could travel by day or night. Neither the pillar of cloud by day nor the pillar of fire by night left its place in front of the people.

Discuss

1. When you left on your trip, how did you figure out where you were going?

2. The Israelites didn't have maps or travel agents. How did they know where to go?
3. Why didn't God lead them the short way?
4. God wants to lead us just as he led the Israelites. To follow God means to do what he wants us to do in all the choices that we make each day. How can we know what God wants us to do?

Final Thought

God led the Israelites the long way to Canaan because he had many things to teach them in the wilderness. Also, he didn't want them to have to fight the people who lived in the land of the short road. God knows what is best for us. He can see things that we can't see when we are making decisions. That is why it makes sense for us to trust and follow him.

Pray

Heavenly Father, you care about me and want to lead me on the right road every day. Help me to follow you by obeying your Word. In Jesus' name. Amen.

Sing—*Guide Me Ever, Great Redeemer* (p. 193)

Open now the crystal fountain
Where the healing waters flow;
Let the fire and cloudy pillar
Lead me all my journey through.
Strong deliv'rer, strong deliv'rer,
Shield me with your mighty arm,
Shield me with your mighty arm.

Do

Draw a map of the route that you are taking on your trip. Write at the top of the page, "I will follow Jesus." Mount this on the first page of your family vacation scrapbook.

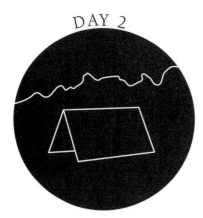

DAY 2

Has your family run into problems yet? The Israelites ran into big problems right away. Pharaoh came after them with his army. With the sea in front of them, mountains on either side, and an army closing in behind, the Israelites found themselves trapped!

Read—*Exodus 14:10–18*

As Pharaoh approached, the Israelites looked up, and there were the Egyptians, marching after them. They were terrified and cried out to the LORD. They said to Moses, "Was it because there were no graves in Egypt that you brought us to the desert to die? What have you done to us by bringing us out of Egypt? Didn't we say to you in Egypt, 'Leave us alone; let us serve the Egyptians'? It would have been better for us to serve the Egyptians than to die in the desert!"

Moses answered the people, "Do not be afraid. Stand firm and you will see the deliverance the LORD will bring you today. The Egyptians you see today you will never see again. The LORD will fight for you; you need only to be still."

Then the LORD said to Moses, "Why are you crying out to me? Tell the Israelites to move on. Raise your staff and stretch out your hand over the sea to divide the water so that the Israelites can go through the sea on dry ground. I will harden the hearts of the Egyptians so that they will go in after them. And I will gain glory through Pharaoh and all his army, through his chariots and his horsemen. The Egyptians will know that I am the LORD when I gain glory through Pharaoh, his chariots and his horsemen."

Discuss

1. How did the Israelites feel when they found that Pharaoh's army was coming after them?
2. What did they say to Moses?
3. How did Moses answer them?

4. What did God tell them to do? How would you have felt about this command if you had been one of the Israelites?

Final Thought

When the pressure is on—that's when we show what kind of people we are and what we really believe. The Israelites panicked and lashed out at Moses. They forgot about God. But what did Moses do? He reminded them of God's promises. When we feel panicky, we need to remember that the Lord will fight for us. We simply need to be still, quietly trusting in him and listening for his voice.

Pray

Dear Lord, thank you that there is nothing too difficult for you. Help me to trust in you when I'm in big trouble. In Jesus' name. Amen.

Sing—*Guide Me Ever, Great Redeemer* (p. 193)

When I tread the verge of Jordan,
Bid my anxious fears subside;
Death of death and hell's destruction,
Land me safe on Canaan's side.
Songs and praises, songs and praises,
I will raise forevermore,
I will raise forevermore.

Do

Write on a slip of paper what you want to remember when a problem comes up. Mount this in your vacation scrapbook, leaving room for a photo. When a problem comes, such as a flat tire, a spilled Coke, or a motel with no vacancies, take a picture that you can mount under your reminder. This way, you can look at problems as opportunities to trust the Lord.

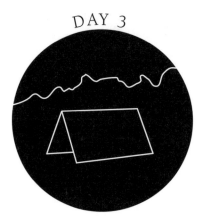

DAY 3

Yesterday we read about the problems the Israelites faced at the beginning of their trip. Do you remember what their situation was? Today we read the continuation of that story.

Read—*Exodus 14:19–31*

Then the angel of God, who had been traveling in front of Israel's army, withdrew and went behind them. The pillar of cloud also moved from in front and stood behind them, coming between the armies of Egypt and Israel. Throughout the night the cloud brought darkness to the one side and light to the other side; so neither went near the other all night long.

Then Moses stretched out his hand over the sea, and all that night the LORD drove the sea back with a strong east wind and turned it into dry land. The waters were divided, and the Israelites went through the sea on dry ground, with a wall of water on their right and on their left.

The Egyptians pursued them, and all Pharaoh's horses and chariots and horsemen followed them into the sea. During the last watch of the night the LORD looked down from the pillar of fire and cloud at the Egyptian army and threw it into confusion. He made the wheels of their chariots come off so that they had difficulty driving. And the Egyptians said, "Let's get away from the Israelites! The LORD is fighting for them against Egypt."

Then the LORD said to Moses, "Stretch out your hand over the sea so that the waters may flow back over the Egyptians and their chariots and horsemen." Moses stretched out his hand over the sea, and at daybreak the sea went back to its place. The Egyptians were fleeing toward it, and the LORD swept them into the sea. The water flowed back and covered the chariots and horsemen—the entire army of Pharaoh that had followed the Israelites into the sea. Not one of them survived.

But the Israelites went through the sea on dry ground, with a wall of water on their right and on their left. That day the LORD saved

Israel from the hands of the Egyptians, and Israel saw the Egyptians lying dead on the shore. And when the Israelites saw the great power the LORD displayed against the Egyptians, the people feared the LORD and put their trust in him and in Moses his servant.

Discuss

1. What are some of the special things that God did to save the Israelites?
2. What happened to Pharaoh's army?
3. When the Israelites saw God's great power, what did they do?
4. What does this show us about God?

Final Thought

Even though the Israelites had a big problem, God showed that he was much bigger than their problem. This is easy to forget when problems arise. Yet God can help us in a mighty way, just as he did the Israelites.

Pray

Almighty God, help us to remember to trust you instead of becoming worried and upset. In Jesus' name. Amen.

Sing—*Guide Me Ever, Great Redeemer* (p. 193)

Open now the crystal fountain
Where the healing waters flow;
Let the fire and cloudy pillar
Lead me all my journey through.
Strong deliv'rer, strong deliv'rer,
Shield me with your mighty arm,
Shield me with your mighty arm.

Do

Begin a record of problems you encounter and how God helps you. Add this to your vacation scrapbook.

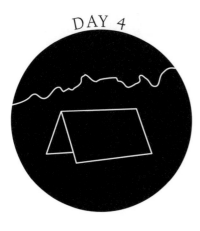

DAY 4

Do you ever get thirsty when you are driving in the car on a long trip? How about on a long hike? When our family goes camping, we often hike for five or six hours a day. Once we carried only one canteen for the four of us to share on a hot, long hike in the highlands of Nova Scotia. We had to ration out the water so that we didn't run out. Fortunately, blueberries grew everywhere and eating the blueberries helped to satisfy our thirst. Imagine not having anything to drink for three whole days.

Read—*Exodus 15:22–27*

Then Moses led Israel from the Red Sea and they went into the Desert of Shur. For three days they traveled in the desert without finding water. When they came to Marah, they could not drink its water because it was bitter. (That is why the place is called Marah.) So the people grumbled against Moses, saying, "What are we to drink?"

Then Moses cried out to the LORD, and the LORD showed him a piece of wood. He threw it into the water, and the water became sweet.

There the LORD made a decree and a law for them, and there he tested them. He said, "If you listen carefully to the voice of the LORD your God and do what is right in his eyes, if you pay attention to his commands and keep all his decrees, I will not bring on you any of the diseases I brought on the Egyptians, for I am the LORD, who heals you."

Then they came to Elim, where there were twelve springs and seventy palm trees, and they camped there near the water.

Discuss

1. What did the Israelites do when they couldn't find any good water to drink?

2. What did Moses do? What did God do?
3. What is grumbling? Do you ever grumble? Does it make your parents happy when you grumble?
4. What do you think God thinks of grumbling? Why?

Final Thought

Think of that bitter water as a problem in your life. When we grumble, we are really saying that God either doesn't care or isn't able to help us. Instead of grumbling, we should pray. When we pray, often God doesn't take our problem away, but he turns it into something good, just like he made the bitter water sweet. Can you think of a problem that God has turned into something good?

Pray

Father, thank you that all good gifts come from you. Help me to pray instead of grumbling. In Jesus' name. Amen.

Sing—*Guide Me Ever, Great Redeemer* (p. 193)

Open now the crystal fountain
Where the healing waters flow;
Let the fire and cloudy pillar
Lead me all my journey through.
Strong deliv'rer, strong deliv'rer,
Shield me with your mighty arm,
Shield me with your mighty arm.

Do

Buy a box of soda crackers and eat as many as you can. Don't drink anything. Wait a little while before you have anything to drink. As you wait, talk about what it was like for the Israelites in the hot desert without anything to drink for three days.

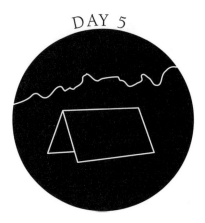

DAY 5

Do you ever ask your parents, "When is it going to be lunchtime?" When you're traveling, it seems that all you can think about is food! The Israelites felt the same way, only worse. There wasn't any fast food in the desert—only sand!

Read—*Exodus 16:2–8*

In the desert the whole community grumbled against Moses and Aaron. The Israelites said to them, "If only we had died by the LORD's hand in Egypt! There we sat around pots of meat and ate all the food we wanted, but you have brought us out into this desert to starve this entire assembly to death."

Then the LORD said to Moses, "I will rain down bread from heaven for you. The people are to go out each day and gather enough for that day. In this way I will test them and see whether they will follow my instructions. On the sixth day they are to prepare what they bring in, and that is to be twice as much as they gather on the other days."

So Moses and Aaron said to all the Israelites, "In the evening you will know that it was the LORD who brought you out of Egypt, and in the morning you will see the glory of the LORD, because he has heard your grumbling against him. Who are we, that you should grumble against us?" Moses also said, "You will know that it was the LORD when he gives you meat to eat in the evening and all the bread you want in the morning, because he has heard your grumbling against him. Who are we? You are not grumbling against us, but against the LORD."

Discuss

1. What were the Israelites grumbling about?
2. Whom did Moses say they were really complaining against?
3. Why did he say that?

4. When we complain to our parents, whom are we really complaining against? Is it wrong to complain? Why?

Final Thought

Complaining is one of our favorite pastimes. It comes naturally to us because we are all sinners. Yet in Philippians 2:14, God commands us to "do everything without complaining or arguing." Why? Because complaining is the mark of people who don't trust God.

If we trust God, we have no reason to complain. We know that our lives are safe in his hands.

Pray

Dear Lord, help us to believe in you and not to complain. Make us more like Moses and less like the Israelites. In Jesus' name. Amen.

Sing—*Guide Me Ever, Great Redeemer* (p. 193)

Guide me ever, great Redeemer,
Pilgrim through this barren land.
I am weak, but you are mighty;
Hold me with your pow'rful hand.
Bread of heaven, bread of heaven,
Feed me now and evermore,
Feed me now and evermore.

Do

Think of a secret signal for your family members to remind each other not to complain. Then make a commitment that you will try never to complain and that you will help each other in this as well. Write down your commitment and have all your family members sign it. Put this in your vacation scrapbook.

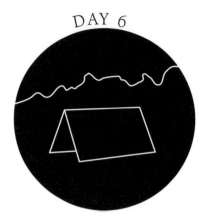

DAY 6

Do you remember yesterday's discussion about grumbling? Why were the Israelites unhappy? Today we will see what God did about their situation.

Read—*Exodus 16:9–18, 31*

Then Moses told Aaron, "Say to the entire Israelite community, 'Come before the LORD, for he has heard your grumbling.'"

While Aaron was speaking to the whole Israelite community, they looked toward the desert, and there was the glory of the LORD appearing in the cloud. The LORD said to Moses, "I have heard the grumbling of the Israelites. Tell them, 'At twilight you will eat meat, and in the morning you will be filled with bread. Then you will know that I am the LORD your God.'"

That evening quail came and covered the camp, and in the morning there was a layer of dew around the camp. When the dew was gone, thin flakes like frost on the ground appeared on the desert floor. When the Israelites saw it, they said to each other, "What is it?" For they did not know what it was.

Moses said to them, "It is the bread the LORD has given you to eat. This is what the LORD has commanded: 'Each one is to gather as much as he needs. Take an omer for each person you have in your tent.'"

The Israelites did as they were told; some gathered much, some little. And when they measured it by the omer, he who gathered much did not have too much, and he who gathered little did not have too little. Each one gathered as much as he needed. . . .

The people of Israel called the bread manna. It was white like coriander seed and tasted like wafers made with honey.

Discuss

1. When the Israelites were hungry, how did the Lord provide for their needs?
2. What did the manna look and taste like?

3. What did the Lord want the Israelites to learn and remember from this miracle?
4. Can you think of some wonderful ways that God has given you or your family just what you needed?

Final Thought

God gave the Israelites the amount of food that they needed, not more, not less. He has promised us that he will give us everything that we need. As we get to know God better and we see how he takes care of us in all sorts of situations, we learn to trust and respect God. When a need arises, we remember how he took care of us in the past and we know that he will take care of us again. This helps us to trust in him rather than complaining or worrying.

Pray

Dear Lord, help us to remember that you are the Lord our God. You love us and provide for us. Thank you. In Jesus' name. Amen.

Sing—*All People That on Earth Do Dwell* (p. 204)

Know that the Lord is God indeed;
Without our aid he did us make.
We are his folk, he doth us feed,
And for his sheep he doth us take.

Do

Write a list of some of the good things that God has given you. You may limit it to blessings you have received while on vacation, or you may make it more general. Think of a title for your list and mount this in your scrapbook.

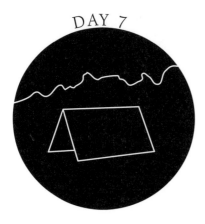

DAY 7

Last summer when we were camping, Laura was twice attacked by angry bees. Without knowing it, we had disturbed their nest. They stung her arms, legs, even her eyelid! The Israelites found themselves being attacked, not by bees, but by a group of people called the Amalekites. Moses chose a young man named Joshua to lead the Israelite men in battle. He knew that his place was not on the battlefield. Moses had a more important job to do.

Read—*Exodus 17:8–15*

The Amalekites came and attacked the Israelites at Rephidim. Moses said to Joshua, "Choose some of our men and go out to fight the Amalekites. Tomorrow I will stand on top of the hill with the staff of God in my hands."

So Joshua fought the Amalekites as Moses had ordered, and Moses, Aaron and Hur went to the top of the hill. As long as Moses held up his hands, the Israelites were winning, but whenever he lowered his hands, the Amalekites were winning. When Moses' hands grew tired, they took a stone and put it under him and he sat on it. Aaron and Hur held his hands up—one on one side, one on the other—so that his hands remained steady till sunset. So Joshua overcame the Amalekite army with the sword.

Then the LORD said to Moses, "Write this on a scroll as something to be remembered and make sure that Joshua hears it, because I will completely blot out the memory of Amalek from under heaven."

Moses built an altar and called it The LORD is my Banner.

Discuss

1. Where did Moses go during the fighting? Why?
2. What happened when Moses' hands or arms got tired?

3. What lessons do you think God wanted Moses and the Israelites to learn from this?
4. How can we be like Moses when we have problems and struggles? What does God want us to do?

Final Thought

Sometimes we get tired or sick or discouraged. At times like this, it is hard to pray. This is when our Christian friendships are especially important. Just like Aaron and Hur, our friends can support us by praying for us. To pray for friends in need is the best thing we can do for them. We must simply lay their problems at Jesus' feet. He alone knows what is best for them.

Pray

Heavenly Father, thank you for giving us Christian friends who can pray for us when we are tired and discouraged. In Jesus' name. Amen.

Sing—*What a Friend We Have in Jesus* (p. 200)

Have we trials and temptations?
Is there trouble anywhere?
We should never be discouraged—
Take it to the Lord in prayer.
Can we find a friend so faithful
Who will all our sorrows share?
Jesus knows our ev'ry weakness—
Take it to the Lord in prayer.

Do

Have each person think of one special friend with whom he or she can share problems and who can pray for him or her. Write down the name and/or draw a picture of this special Christian friend.

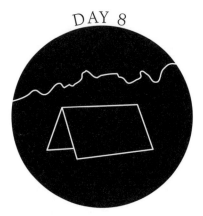

DAY 8

Once when our family was camping on top of a mountain, we found ourselves in the middle of a thunderstorm. We were literally in the clouds, and the lightning flashed and the thunder crashed around us. We were terrified! Try to imagine what it must have been like for Moses and the Israelites when God met them at Mount Sinai.

Read—*Exodus 19:3–9, 16–19*

Then Moses went up to God, and the LORD called to him from the mountain and said, "This is what you are to say to the house of Jacob and what you are to tell the people of Israel: 'You yourselves have seen what I did to Egypt, and how I carried you on eagles' wings and brought you to myself. Now if you obey me fully and keep my covenant, then out of all nations you will be my treasured possession. Although the whole earth is mine, you will be for me a kingdom of priests and a holy nation.' These are the words you are to speak to the Israelites."

So Moses went back and summoned the elders of the people and set before them all the words the LORD had commanded him to speak. The people all responded together, "We will do everything the LORD has said." So Moses brought their answer back to the LORD.

The LORD said to Moses, "I am going to come to you in a dense cloud, so that the people will hear me speaking with you and will always put their trust in you." Then Moses told the LORD what the people had said. . . .

On the morning of the third day there was thunder and lightning, with a thick cloud over the mountain, and a very loud trumpet blast. Everyone in the camp trembled. Then Moses led the people out of the camp to meet with God, and they stood at the foot of the mountain. Mount Sinai was covered with smoke, because the LORD descended on it in fire. The smoke billowed up from it like smoke from a furnace, the whole mountain trembled violently, and the sound of the trumpet grew louder and louder. Then Moses spoke and the voice of God answered him.

Discuss

1. What "special effects" did God use when he came to Moses?
2. Why did God use "special effects?" (Hint: God told Moses why.)
3. What did God tell Moses that he would do if the people obeyed him?
4. Why is it important for us to obey God?

Final Thought

God called Moses up on the mountain to give him the law. He was going to tell Moses all the things that the Israelites should and shouldn't do. One of the reasons God came in such a loud, powerful thunderstorm was to show the people that he was there and he was telling Moses what to write down. Moses wasn't just making it up himself.

Pray

Holy Father, you are a mighty God. Even the loudest, most frightening thunderstorm is nothing compared to your great power. Yet you love us and have made us your own—your treasured possession. Thank you for your love. Help us to honor and obey your Word. In Jesus' name. Amen.

Sing—*Oh, Worship the King* (pp. 190–91)

Oh, tell of his might; oh, sing of his grace,
Whose robe is the light, whose canopy space;
His chariots of wrath the deep thunderclouds form,
And dark is his path on the wings of the storm.

Do

Draw a picture of the thunderstorm on the mountain. Put these pictures in your vacation scrapbook.

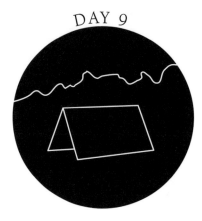

DAY 9

Do you remember yesterday's story of the thunderstorm on Mount Sinai? Today we read about the important message God gave Moses on the mountaintop.

Read—*Exodus 20:1–18*

And God spoke all these words:

"I am the LORD your God, who brought you out of Egypt, out of the land of slavery.

"You shall have no other gods before me.

"You shall not make for yourself an idol in the form of anything in heaven above or on the earth beneath or in the waters below. You shall not bow down to them or worship them; for I, the LORD your God, am a jealous God, punishing the children for the sin of the fathers to the third and fourth generation of those who hate me, but showing love to a thousand generations of those who love me and keep my commandments.

"You shall not misuse the name of the LORD your God, for the LORD will not hold anyone guiltless who misuses his name.

"Remember the Sabbath day by keeping it holy. Six days you shall labor and do all your work, but the seventh day is a Sabbath to the LORD your God. On it you shall not do any work, neither you, nor your son or daughter, nor your manservant or maidservant, nor your animals, nor the alien within your gates. For in six days the LORD made the heavens and the earth, the sea, and all that is in them, but he rested on the seventh day. Therefore the LORD blessed the Sabbath day and made it holy.

"Honor your father and your mother, so that you may live long in the land the LORD your God is giving you.

"You shall not murder.

"You shall not commit adultery.

"You shall not steal.

"You shall not give false testimony against your neighbor.

"You shall not covet your neighbor's house. You shall not covet your neighbor's wife, or his manservant or maidservant, his ox or donkey, or anything that belongs to your neighbor."

When the people saw the thunder and lightning and heard the trumpet and saw the mountain in smoke, they trembled with fear.

Discuss

1. The first five commandments have to do with respecting God. The last five have to do with respecting other people. What does it mean to respect someone?
2. Why is this so important?
3. How do you show respect for God? Your family? Others?
4. What sorts of things do you do that are disrespectful? What can you do differently?

Final Thought

One rule in our family is "No put-downs." Put-down humor has no place in the Christian home. It kills respect, and God wants us to honor each other because we are made in his image.

Pray

Heavenly Father, help us to honor you in everything we do and say. Help us to show respect for others, especially those in our own family. In Jesus' name. Amen.

Sing—*O Word of God Incarnate* (p. 194)

O Word of God incarnate,
O Wisdom from on high,
O Truth unchanged, unchanging,
O Light of our dark sky:

We praise you for the radiance
That from the hallowed page,
A lantern to our footsteps,
Shines on from age to age.

Do

If you were going to make ten rules for your family to live by, what would they be? Write down your family's own "Ten Commandments" and mount them in your scrapbook.

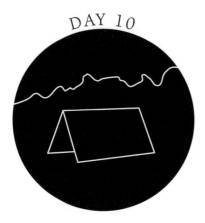

DAY 10

Moses was gone so long that the people thought he would never come back. They asked Moses' brother Aaron to make them another god to lead them. Aaron made them a golden calf. The Lord was so angry that he told Moses that he would destroy the entire nation. When Moses came down from the mountain, the people were worshiping the calf by throwing a wild party.

Read—*Exodus 32:19–26, 30–34*

When Moses approached the camp and saw the calf and the dancing, his anger burned and he threw the tablets out of his hands, breaking them to pieces at the foot of the mountain. And he took the calf they had made and burned it in the fire; then he ground it to powder, scattered it on the water and made the Israelites drink it.

He said to Aaron, "What did these people do to you, that you led them into such great sin?"

"Do not be angry, my lord," Aaron answered. "You know how prone these people are to evil. They said to me, 'Make us gods who will go before us. As for this fellow Moses who brought us up out of Egypt, we don't know what has happened to him.' So I told them, 'Whoever has any gold jewelry, take it off.' Then they gave me the gold, and I threw it into the fire, and out came this calf!"

Moses saw that the people were running wild and that Aaron had let them get out of control and so become a laughingstock to their enemies. So he stood at the entrance to the camp and said, "Whoever is for the LORD, come to me. . . ."

The next day Moses said to the people, "You have committed a great sin. But now I will go up to the LORD; perhaps I can make atonement for your sin."

So Moses went back to the LORD and said, "Oh, what a great sin these people have committed! They have made themselves gods of

gold. But now, please forgive their sin—but if not, then blot me out
of the book you have written."

The LORD replied to Moses, "Whoever has sinned against me I will
blot out of my book. Now go, lead the people to the place I spoke
of, and my angel will go before you. However, when the time comes
for me to punish, I will punish them for their sin."

Discuss

1. What did Moses do when he saw the calf and the dancing?
2. Even though Moses was terribly angry with the people, he
   prayed for them, asking God not to destroy them. Read his
   prayer.
3. What did he offer to do? Why do you think he offered this?

Final Thought

Moses could not die for the Israelites' sin, because he, like the
Israelites, was sinful. Only the death of God's perfect Son, Jesus
Christ, could remove sin.

Pray

Dear Lord, thank you that because of Jesus' death on the cross,
you forgive me and take away my sin. In Jesus' name. Amen.

Sing—*Before You, Lord, We Bow* (p. 207)

Earth, hear your Maker's voice;
Your great Redeemer own;
Believe, obey, rejoice,
And worship him alone.
Cast down your pride, your sin deplore,
And bow before the Crucified.

Do

Write down a sin that you are ashamed of, then rip the paper up.
Burn or throw away the pieces, thanking God for his forgiveness.

DAY 11

Think back over the past week. Was there a time when you disobeyed your parents? We all disobey God. As great a leader as Moses was, even he disobeyed God.

Read—*Numbers 20:2–12*

Now there was no water for the community, and the people gathered in opposition to Moses and Aaron. They quarreled with Moses and said, "If only we had died when our brothers fell dead before the LORD! Why did you bring the LORD's community into this desert, that we and our livestock should die here? Why did you bring us up out of Egypt to this terrible place? It has no grain or figs, grapevines or pomegranates. And there is no water to drink!"

Moses and Aaron went from the assembly to the entrance to the Tent of Meeting and fell facedown, and the glory of the LORD appeared to them. The LORD said to Moses, "Take the staff, and you and your brother Aaron gather the assembly together. Speak to that rock before their eyes and it will pour out its water. You will bring water out of the rock for the community so they and their livestock can drink."

So Moses took the staff from the LORD's presence, just as he commanded him. He and Aaron gathered the assembly together in front of the rock and Moses said to them, "Listen, you rebels, must we bring you water out of this rock?" Then Moses raised his arm and struck the rock twice with his staff. Water gushed out, and the community and their livestock drank.

But the LORD said to Moses and Aaron, "Because you did not trust in me enough to honor me as holy in the sight of the Israelites, you will not bring this community into the land I give them."

Discuss

1. What right things did Moses do?
2. Where did he go wrong?

3. What was Moses' punishment for disobeying God?
4. Do you think that this was a hard punishment for Moses? Why do you think God punished Moses so severely?

Final Thought

When Moses hit the rock, he did not show respect for God. He acted as if he didn't believe that God could bring water out of the rock in the way that he said he would. Also, the people probably thought that it was Moses who brought water out of the rock. Moses said, "Must we bring you water out of this rock?" (v. 10).

Sometimes when God wants us to do something, we "sort of" obey him. We do something like what he wants us to, but we do it in our own way. Do you think there is such a thing as "sort of" obeying? Why does this make God unhappy? It does not honor God, and God takes this sin very seriously.

Pray

Heavenly Father, we are sorry for losing our tempers and for doing things our own way, instead of obeying you. Forgive us, and help us to remember to honor you. In Jesus' name. Amen.

Sing—*O Word of God Incarnate* (p. 194)

Oh, make your Church, dear Savior,
A lamp of burnished gold
To bear before the nations
Your true light, as of old;
Oh, teach your wand'ring pilgrims
By this their path to trace,
Till, clouds and darkness ended,
They see you face to face.

Do

Find a rock and a stick. Place these out somewhere as a reminder to obey God and not to lose your temper.

DAY 12

As the end of vacation draws near, we read about the end of Moses' life, just before Israel entered the promised land.

Read—*Deuteronomy 32:46–47; 34:1, 4–7, 10–12*

[Moses] said to them, "Take to heart all the words I have solemnly declared to you this day, so that you may command your children to obey carefully all the words of this law. They are not just idle words for you—they are your life. By them you will live long in the land you are crossing the Jordan to possess. . . ."

Then Moses climbed Mount Nebo from the plains of Moab to the top of Pisgah, across from Jericho. There the LORD showed him the whole land—from Gilead to Dan, . . . Then the LORD said to him, "This is the land I promised on oath to Abraham, Isaac and Jacob when I said, 'I will give it to your descendants.' I have let you see it with your eyes, but you will not cross over into it."

And Moses the servant of the LORD died there in Moab, as the LORD had said. He buried him in Moab, in the valley opposite Beth Peor, but to this day no one knows where his grave is. Moses was a hundred and twenty years old when he died, yet his eyes were not weak nor his strength gone. . . .

Since then, no prophet has risen in Israel like Moses, whom the LORD knew face to face, who did all those miraculous signs and wonders the LORD sent him to do in Egypt—to Pharaoh and to all his officials and to his whole land. For no one has ever shown the mighty power or performed the awesome deeds that Moses did in the sight of all Israel.

Discuss

1. Before he died, what did Moses say about obeying God?
2. How do you think Moses felt when he looked out and saw the land that he had been trying to get to for forty years?

3. How did Moses die? Who buried him?

4. What do the last three verses say about Moses? Would you like to be like Moses? In what way?

Final Thought

God kept his promise not to let Moses enter the new land because Moses disobeyed him. But God did answer Moses' prayer and let him see the new land. When we trust in Jesus as our Savior, we enter the promised land of God's family. And one day we will be home with him in heaven. That is the perfect home, where everyone loves each other and everything is exactly right. As you return home, remember that your true home is in heaven!

Pray

Father, you are gracious and good. Thank you for caring for us, just as you cared for Moses and the Israelites. We sin and complain and lose our tempers just as they did, yet you forgive our sin. Because of Jesus, we can one day enter heaven. We thank and praise you, Lord, in Jesus' name. Amen.

Sing—*Guide Me Ever, Great Redeemer* (p. 193)

When I tread the verge of Jordan,
Bid my anxious fears subside;
Death of death and hell's destruction,
Land me safe on Canaan's side.
Songs and praises, songs and praises,
I will raise forevermore,
I will raise forevermore.

Do

Remember together all the good things that the Lord has done for you on your vacation.

FAMILY WORSHIP
FOR VACATION

Vacations often present the opportunity for family worship. Worship is a celebration of who God is and what he has done. The following family worship times focus on Moses' face-to-face encounters with God. The goal of this time is to draw the family into a face-to-face encounter with the glory of God.

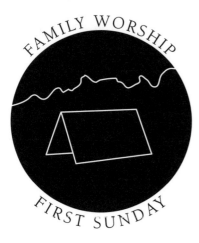

Call to Worship—
Deuteronomy 32:3–4

Leader 1

I will proclaim the name of the
    LORD.
    Oh, praise the greatness of our
      God!
He is the Rock, his works are perfect,
    and all his ways are just.
A faithful God who does no
      wrong,
    upright and just is he.

Sing—*Praise, My Soul, the King of Heaven* (p. 191)

Praise, my soul, the King of heaven;
To his feet your tribute bring.
Ransomed, healed, restored, forgiven,
Evermore his praises sing.
Alleluia! Alleluia!
Praise the everlasting King!

Praise him for his grace and favor
To our forebears in distress.
Praise him, still the same forever,
Slow to chide and swift to bless.
Alleluia! Alleluia!
Glorious in his faithfulness!

Tenderly he shields and spares us;
Well our feeble frame he knows.
In his hands he gently bears us,
Rescues us from all our foes.
Alleluia! Alleluia!
Widely as his mercy flows.

Angels help us to adore him,
Who behold him face to face.

Sun and moon bow down before him;
All who dwell in time and space.
Alleluia! Alleluia!
Praise with us the God of grace.

Responsive Reading—*Psalm 136*

Leader 1:   Give thanks to the Lord, for he is good.
All: His love endures forever.

Leader 2:   Give thanks to the God of gods.
All: His love endures forever.

Leader 1:   Give thanks to the Lord of lords:
All: His love endures forever.

Leader 2:   to him who alone does great wonders,
All: His love endures forever.

Leader 1:   who by his understanding made the heavens,
All: His love endures forever.

Leader 2:   who spread out the earth upon the waters,
All: His love endures forever.

Leader 1:   who made the great lights—
All: His love endures forever.

Leader 2:   the sun to govern the day,
All: His love endures forever.

Leader 1:   the moon and stars to govern the night;
All: His love endures forever.

Leader 2:   to him who struck down the firstborn of Egypt
All: His love endures forever.

Leader 1:   and brought Israel out from among them
All: His love endures forever.

Leader 2:   with a mighty hand and outstretched arm;
All: His love endures forever.

Leader 1:   to him who divided the Red Sea asunder
All: His love endures forever.

Leader 2:   and brought Israel through the midst of it,
All: His love endures forever.

Leader 1:   but swept Pharaoh and his army into the Red Sea;
All: His love endures forever.

Leader 2:   to him who led his people through the desert,
All: His love endures forever.

Leader 1:   who struck down great kings,
All: His love endures forever.

Leader 2:   and killed mighty kings—
All: His love endures forever.

Leader 1:   Sihon king of the Amorites
All: His love endures forever.

Leader 2:   and Og king of Bashan—
All: His love endures forever.

Leader 1:   and gave their land as an inheritance,
All: His love endures forever.

Leader 2:   an inheritance to his servant Israel
All: His love endures forever.

Leader 1:   to the One who remembered us in our low estate
All: His love endures forever.

Leader 2:   and freed us from our enemies,
All: His love endures forever.

Leader 1:   and who gives food to every creature.
All: His love endures forever.

Leader 2:   Give thanks to the God of heaven.
All: His love endures forever.

Old Testament Reading—*Exodus 33:12–23*

Moses said to the LORD, "You have been telling me, 'Lead these people,' but you have not let me know whom you will send with me. You have said, 'I know you by name and you have found favor with me.' If you are pleased with me, teach me your ways so I may know you and continue to find favor with you. Remember that this nation is your people."

The LORD replied, "My Presence will go with you, and I will give you rest."

Then Moses said to him, "If your Presence does not go with us, do not send us up from here. How will anyone know that you are pleased with me and with your people unless you go with us? What else will distinguish me and your people from all the other people on the face of the earth?"

And the LORD said to Moses, "I will do the very thing you have asked, because I am pleased with you and I know you by name."

Then Moses said, "Now show me your glory."

And the LORD said, "I will cause all my goodness to pass in front of you, and I will proclaim my name, the LORD, in your presence. I will have mercy on whom I will have mercy, and I will have compassion on whom I will have compassion. But," he said, "you cannot see my face, for no one may see me and live."

Then the LORD said, "There is a place near me where you may stand on a rock. When my glory passes by, I will put you in a cleft in the rock and cover you with my hand until I have passed by. Then I will remove my hand and you will see my back; but my face must not be seen."

New Testament Reading—*Mark 9:2–8*

After six days Jesus took Peter, James and John with him and led them up a high mountain, where they were all alone. There he was transfigured before them. His clothes became dazzling white, whiter than anyone in the world could bleach them. And there appeared before them Elijah and Moses, who were talking with Jesus.

Peter said to Jesus, "Rabbi, it is good for us to be here. Let us put up three shelters—one for you, one for Moses and one for Elijah." (He did not know what to say, they were so frightened.)

Then a cloud appeared and enveloped them, and a voice came from the cloud: "This is my Son, whom I love. Listen to him!"

Suddenly, when they looked around, they no longer saw anyone with them except Jesus.

Discuss

1. What did Moses pray for? Why?
2. What was God's answer?
3. Why wasn't Moses allowed to see God's face?
4. Did Moses ever see God's face? When?

Final Thought

The Bible tells us that God has shown himself to us in Jesus (Col. 1:15–20). Jesus shows us exactly what God is like. Do you want to see God face-to-face, as Moses did? How can we do that?

Pray

Holy Father, we praise you for your glory. Thank you for showing yourself to us in Jesus. Because of his death on the cross, we can know you and speak to you face-to-face, as Moses did. In Jesus' name we pray. Amen.

Sing—*Immortal, Invisible, God Only Wise* (p. 195)

Immortal, invisible, God only wise,
In light inaccessible hid from our eyes,
Most blessed, most glorious, the Ancient of Days,
Almighty, victorious, thy great name we praise!

Thou reignest in glory; thou dwellest in light;
Thine angels adore thee, all veiling their sight;
All laud we would render; oh, help us to see
'Tis only the splendor of light hideth thee!

Call to Worship— *Psalm 29:1–2*

Leader

Ascribe to the LORD, O mighty ones,
    ascribe to the LORD glory and
      strength.
Ascribe to the LORD the glory due his
    name;
    worship the LORD in the splendor
      of his holiness.

Pray

Heavenly Father, you are great and mighty. We see your works around us and give you humble praise. Enable us to worship you now, in Jesus' name. Amen.

Sing—*Oh, Worship the King* (pp. 190–91)

Oh, worship the King, all-glorious above.
Oh, gratefully sing his pow'r and his love;
Our shield and defender, the Ancient of Days,
Pavilioned in splendor, and girded with praise.

Oh, tell of his might; oh, sing of his grace,
Whose robe is the light, whose canopy space;
His chariots of wrath the deep thunderclouds form,
And dark is his path on the wings of the storm.

The earth with its store of wonders untold,
Almighty, your pow'r has founded of old;
Established it fast by a changeless decree,
And round it has cast, like a mantle, the sea.

Your bountiful care what tongue can recite?
It breathes in the air, it shines in the light,
It streams from the hills, it descends to the plain,
And sweetly distills in the dew and the rain.

Frail children of dust, and feeble as frail,
In you do we trust, nor find you to fail;
Your mercies, how tender, how firm to the end,
Our maker, defender, redeemer, and friend.

Responsive Reading—*Psalm 98*

(Note: For families with children not yet reading age, simply have the children respond "Praise the Lord" after each verse. Use a nod for their cue to respond.)

Reader 1: Sing to the LORD a new song,
for he has done marvelous things;
his right hand and his holy arm
have worked salvation for him.

Reader 2: The LORD has made his salvation known
and revealed his righteousness to the nations.

Reader 3: He has remembered his love
and his faithfulness to the house of Israel;
all the ends of the earth have seen
the salvation of our God.

Reader 1: Shout for joy to the LORD, all the earth,
burst into jubilant song with music;

Reader 2: make music to the LORD with the harp,
with the harp and the sound of singing,

Reader 3: with trumpets and the blast of the ram's horn—
shout for joy before the LORD, the King.

Reader 1: Let the sea resound, and everything in it,
the world, and all who live in it.

Reader 2: Let the rivers clap their hands,
let the mountains sing together for joy;

Reader 3: let them sing before the LORD,
for he comes to judge the earth.
He will judge the world in righteousness
and the peoples with equity.

Pray

Lord, we confess that we have sinned against you as the Israelites did. We have disobeyed you in our thoughts, in our words, and in the things that we have done. Forgive us, Lord, for the sake of your Son Jesus Christ, who died in our place, and who lives and rules with you in heaven. Amen.

Old Testament Reading—*Exodus 34:29–35*

When Moses came down from Mount Sinai with the two tablets of the Testimony in his hands, he was not aware that his face was radiant because he had spoken with the LORD. When Aaron and all the Israelites saw Moses, his face was radiant, and they were afraid to come near him. But Moses called to them; so Aaron and all the leaders of the community came back to him, and he spoke to them. Afterward all the Israelites came near him, and he gave them all the commands the LORD had given him on Mount Sinai.

When Moses finished speaking to them, he put a veil over his face. But whenever he entered the LORD's presence to speak with him, he removed the veil until he came out. And when he came out and told the Israelites what he had been commanded, they saw that his face was radiant. Then Moses would put the veil back over his face until he went in to speak with the LORD.

New Testament Reading—*2 Corinthians 3:13–18*

We are not like Moses, who would put a veil over his face to keep the Israelites from gazing at it while the radiance was fading away. But their minds were made dull, for to this day the same veil remains when the old covenant is read. It has not been removed, because only in Christ is it taken away. Even to this day when Moses is read, a veil covers their hearts. But whenever anyone turns to the Lord, the veil is taken away. Now the Lord is the Spirit, and where the Spirit of the Lord is, there is freedom. And we, who with unveiled faces all reflect the Lord's glory, are being transformed into his likeness with ever-increasing glory, which comes from the Lord, who is the Spirit.

Discuss

1. What strange thing happened to Moses' face after he spoke with the Lord? Why do you think this happened?
2. What did Moses wear on his face sometimes? When did he wear it and when did he take it off?
3. The New Testament reading tells us why Moses wore the veil. What didn't Moses want the Israelites to see? Why?
4. How are we like Moses? How are we different from Moses?

Meditation

Our family huddled in a cluster to keep warm against the whipping winds atop Cadillac Mountain. Other families and groups of friends milled about in the gathering twilight. To the east was the deepening gray-blue of sea and sky, but we were facing west. The mountains spread out in undulating black mounds. Wisps of clouds crowned their peaks. As the sun lowered, the crowd settled on the ground and waited, watching silently. It was just like the Fourth of July, only this time it was God's fireworks we were gathering to watch.

We oohed and aahed as the sun transformed the clouds from white to pink to gray-lavender. Then it slipped behind a cloud and sank. The rim of the cloud turned liquid gold. The sun disappeared from sight altogether, and we thought that the sunset was over. Suddenly it dropped from the bottom of the cloud. For a few glorious moments, the sun blazed out between the cloud and the mountaintop—an encore performance. Then it took its final bow and disappeared behind a curtain of mountaintop. The crowd clapped and cheered. It had been a performance of unspeakable beauty.

As lovely as this sunset was, no sunset could hold a candle to God's glory. The glory that Moses got a glimmer of on the mountain was enough to change his appearance the way the setting sun bathes a cloud in pink and gold. Yet, just like the sunset on the mountain, the glory faded from Moses' face. The change didn't last; it was temporary. When Moses spent time talking to God in his house, his face regained that divine glow. But after he was out and about with the people for a while, the sunshine on his face faded and he looked no different from anyone else.

I am like Moses sometimes, aren't you? There are those special times when I feel so close to God—at a wonderful church service, praying with friends, or talking silently with God as I look around at his beautiful creation. In these moments, my heart glows with his presence. But it seems that after a little while, when I'm back to the usual grind of life, that glow is simply a memory. Instead of being loving and gentle, I snap at my family or complain about some silly inconvenience.

In the passage from 2 Corinthians, Paul tells us that yes, we are like Moses in that we do reflect God's glory. But we are different from Moses. Our glory does not fade as Moses' glory did. It doesn't? It feels like it fades. But we can't trust our feelings. The glory that shines out from us doesn't come from anything we do. We may spend many hours at church or in prayer and feel very holy, but that does not make us shine with God's glory.

Where then does the glory come from? It comes from God's very presence living within us in the person of the Holy Spirit. When we ask Jesus to come into our hearts, he makes his home within our lives. The Holy Spirit is the invisible presence of Jesus. And he will never go away, so we don't need to worry about that glory fading away.

In fact, the glory shines from us more and more. Paul tells us that we are slowly being changed by the Holy Spirit so that we are less like our old, sinful selfish self and more like Jesus. Isn't that the greatest miracle of all? It is easy to imagine God crafting the mountains and the ocean, the lakes and the trees, the clouds and the glittering sunshine. The hardest thing to imagine is that God can change people. But he does. That's his specialty.

Pray

Dear Lord, thank you that bit by bit you are changing us so that we are more and more like Jesus. Help us to cooperate with your Holy Spirit. Give us the desire to love and obey you, and then give us the strength to do it so that we can truly reflect your glory. In Jesus' name. Amen.

Sing—*Joyful, Joyful We Adore Thee* (p. 196)

Joyful, joyful we adore thee,
God of glory, Lord of love!
Hearts unfold like flow'rs before thee,
Praising thee, their sun above.
Melt the clouds of sin and sadness,
Drive the gloom of doubt away.
Giver of immortal gladness,
Fill us with the light of day.

All thy works with joy surround thee,
Earth and heav'n reflect thy rays,
Stars and angels sing around thee,
Center of unbroken praise.
Field and forest, vale and mountain,
Flow'ry meadow, flashing sea,
Chanting bird, and flowing fountain
Call us to rejoice in thee.

Thou art giving and forgiving,
Ever blessing, ever blest,
Well-spring of the joy of living,
Ocean-depth of happy rest!
Thou our Father, Christ our brother,
All who live in love are thine;
Teach us how to love each other,
Lift us to the joy divine!

GOD'S KIND OF LOVE

I groaned as my five-year-old daughter Laura handed me her class list. Off we trooped to the drugstore to buy several boxes of inexpensive valentines.

"Definitely not Barbie and Ken!" I insisted. We finally agreed on a Snoopy theme and made our way to the check-out line, which snaked back into the aisles.

"What a racket!" I thought. "I am only one of millions of mothers standing in line at this very moment, holding her child's hand and clutching cellophane-wrapped boxes of valentines."

While we waited, I glanced through some greeting cards. What promised to be cute, funny Valentine cards on the front held X-rated messages inside! Most of them weren't funny or even seductive. They were just plain gross!

"Why are we celebrating this?" I asked myself. "What do children care about romantic love? And the grown-ups see Valentine's Day as a holiday in honor of sex!"

These reflections prompted me to rethink our family's approach to Valentine's Day. Perhaps we needed to look at this celebration of love from a different angle. After all, God's Word does have a few things to say on the subject.

The Story of Saint Valentine

Where did Valentine's Day originate? To my amazement, I discovered that Saint Valentine was a real person! Not only that, he was a man of God.

The Roman soldiers pushed the priest roughly out the door of the prison into the dawn-washed courtyard. Valentine stood, blinking, as his eyes grew accustomed to the early morning light. It seemed that he had been in that dark prison cell forever. He took a deep breath of the fresh air. It was tinged with a hint of spring. High overhead pairs of birds circled and called to one another. Life beckoned, but he could not answer its call.

Another rough push propelled him toward the center of the courtyard where death awaited him. It was a simple but gruesome instrument, a large, heavy ax. As Valentine proceeded toward the block, the courtyard seemed to fill with familiar faces. He saw the tattered forms of poor people to whom he had ministered. Radiant faces called words of encouragement, faces of those whose sicknesses had been healed by Valentine's gentle care. And all around he recognized individuals who had come to Christ through his faithful witness. He would see them again someday, robed in white, free from the pain and persecution of this earthly life.

The faces vanished. Valentine stood alone before the block, flanked by the soldiers who would administer his sentence. He knelt silently, thinking only of the face he soon would see, the face of his Savior, the Lamb of God.

Valentine lived in Rome in the third century A.D. He was both a pastor and a physician. Little is known about him except that he died for his faith in Christ. The above narrative depicts how I imagine Valentine's death. It is his life and death that we commemorate on February 14.

Where then did the idea of romantic love enter the picture? The notion evolved that birds mated on February 14, the very day that Saint Valentine was honored. As a result, this day came to be associated with lovers and courting couples.

While there certainly is a place for romantic love in God's scheme of things, it cannot compare to the love that Valentine's life exemplified. His sacrificial love mirrors the ultimate love, the love that God showed toward us when he gave his Son as a sacrifice for our sins.

God's Kind of Love

Valentine's Day offers the perfect opportunity to explore as a family what God's Word says about love.

The world identifies physical attraction as love. God's Word gives us a much higher standard. God's kind of love puts the other person's interests before one's own. It involves commitment, commitment that stands the test of time. It is not contingent on the other person's response but continues giving regardless of the response.

We will take the weeks before Valentine's Day to look at four examples of God's kind of love. The first devotional emphasizes the unselfish nature of love by looking at the commitment of Ruth to

Naomi. David's commitment to Jonathan is the subject of the second devotional. The focus of this lesson is on keeping one's promises.

Jesus showed us God's kind of love, both in his life and death and in his teaching. For the last two devotions, we will look at two of Jesus' parables that sketch pictures of perfect love. The parable of the prodigal son (better named the parable of the loving father) describes God's unconditional love for sinners and his forgiveness for those who turn to him. The parable of the good Samaritan shows us that true love for God is demonstrated in acts of love and mercy for those in need.

The Valentine Tree

Actions speak louder than words—especially where love is concerned. I certainly want acts of love, kindness, and thoughtfulness to be the norm in my home, not the exception! This doesn't happen spontaneously, I'm afraid. It takes practice. And what better time to practice love than Valentine's Day?

Make it fun by constructing a Valentine tree. All you need is a tree branch, a pot or vase, and the makings for homemade Valentines. It is a simple project that the whole family will enjoy. Complete instructions are in the resources section at the back of the book.

The Valentine tree is designed to underscore what the Bible says about love by requiring each person to act on what he has learned.

Here's how it works. Place the hearts made out of construction paper in a basket near the Valentine tree. When your child does a special act of love for someone in the family (or outside the family), let the child hang a heart on the Valentine tree. (White yarn works well for hanging the hearts on the branches.)

Young children love to see the bare branches fill up with colorful hearts. Their excitement about the tree will motivate them to do loving deeds. This can become a fun, new Valentine's tradition for your family.

Acts of Love

When my children were younger and I prayed with them each night at bedtime, I always thanked God for specific things about them. That was one way I tried to show appreciation for them on a daily basis. Showing appreciation is an important part of building loving relationships, and it ought to be done daily.

Holidays are opportunities to show appreciation in a more intentional way. Valentine's Day can be a special day for each person in the family to affirm his or her love for the others.

Homemade cards are a favorite in our home. Our children are now old enough to write their own messages. I have a file stuffed with homemade greeting cards from our children. The messages scrawled in a child's script are far more precious to me than anything from the pen of a greeting card writer.

Instead of getting a babysitter and going out on Valentine's Day, you may want to consider having a special dinner at home with the family. Prepare one of your family's favorite meals. Include the entire family in the preparations. It should be everyone's labor of love, not just Mom's. Bring out the linen tablecloth, the good china, and the candlesticks. Candlelight and a lovely table is one way to say "you're special" to the members of your family.

The prayer before the meal can be a time of thanksgiving for the loving relationships in your family. Hold hands around the table and let everyone contribute a short thank-you prayer.

Last night my son Mark wrote a piece about himself for school. I read with gratitude his description of his "loving family." We laughed together about what he didn't describe, like my constant frustration over neglected chores. "Oh, that goes without saying, Mom," he reassured me. He knew that despite our occasional outbursts of anger and frustration, our family loves each other.

Loving relationships are at the heart of God's desire for us. Let's not miss the Valentine's Day opportunity to learn about God's kind of love and to express this love in deeds of kindness and appreciation.

FAMILY DEVOTIONS
FOR VALENTINE'S DAY

Long ago, there was no food to eat in Israel. Naomi, her husband, and her two sons moved to a nearby country called Moab, where there was food to eat. After several years, Naomi's husband and two sons died. Now Naomi had no family left at all, except for the Moabite women whom her sons had married, Orpah and Ruth.

Read—*Ruth 1:6–18*

When she heard in Moab that the LORD had come to the aid of his people by providing food for them, Naomi and her daughters-in-law prepared to return home from there. With her two daughters-in-law she left the place where she had been living and set out on the road that would take them back to the land of Judah.

Then Naomi said to her two daughters-in-law, "Go back, each of you, to your mother's home. May the LORD show kindness to you, as you have shown to your dead and to me. May the LORD grant that each of you will find rest in the home of another husband."

Then she kissed them and they wept aloud and said to her, "We will go back with you to your people."

But Naomi said, "Return home, my daughters. Why would you come with me? Am I going to have any more sons, who could become your husbands? Return home, my daughters; I am too old to have another husband. Even if I thought there was still hope for me—even if I had a husband tonight and then gave birth to sons— would you wait until they grew up? Would you remain unmarried for them? No, my daughters. It is more bitter for me than for you, because the LORD's hand has gone out against me!"

At this they wept again. Then Orpah kissed her mother-in-law good-by, but Ruth clung to her.

"Look," said Naomi, "your sister-in-law is going back to her people and her gods. Go back with her."

But Ruth replied, "Don't urge me to leave you or to turn back from you. Where you go I will go, and where you stay I will stay. Your people will be my people and your God my God. Where you die I will die, and there I will be buried. May the LORD deal with me, be it ever so severely, if anything but death separates you and me." When Naomi realized that Ruth was determined to go with her, she stopped urging her.

Discuss

1. Did Naomi's daughters-in-law love her? How do you know?
2. Which one loved her more? How did she show it?
3. What did Ruth leave in order to be with Naomi?
4. How was Ruth's love for Naomi like Jesus' love for us?

Final Thought

Ruth gave up everything for Naomi. She was unselfish. She didn't think of herself and what would make her happy. Instead she thought of Naomi and what would be best for her. Can you think of ways that you can be unselfish with your family?

Pray

Dear Lord, you left all the riches of heaven to come down and save us. Help us to be unselfish too. In Jesus' name. Amen.

Sing—*The King of Love My Shepherd Is* (p. 201)

The King of love my shepherd is,
Whose goodness faileth never;
I nothing lack if I am his
And he is mine forever.

Do

Do something unselfish this week. Then hang a heart on your Valentine tree.

TWO WEEKS BEFORE VALENTINE'S DAY

Today we will look at the love that David had for his best friend, Jonathan. David had promised Jonathan that he would show kindness to Jonathan's family if Jonathan should die. Sure enough, Jonathan died first, in battle, and David became king of Israel.

Read—2 Samuel 4:4; 9:1–10, 11

(Jonathan son of Saul had a son who was lame in both feet. He was five years old when the news about Saul and Jonathan came from Jezreel. His nurse picked him up and fled, but as she hurried to leave, he fell and became crippled. His name was Mephibosheth.) . . .

David asked, "Is there anyone still left of the house of Saul to whom I can show kindness for Jonathan's sake?"

Now there was a servant of Saul's household named Ziba. They called him to appear before David, and the king said to him, "Are you Ziba?"

"Your servant," he replied.

The king asked, "Is there no one still left of the house of Saul to whom I can show God's kindness?"

Ziba answered the king, "There is still a son of Jonathan; he is crippled in both feet."

"Where is he?" the king asked.

Ziba answered, "He is at the house of Makir son of Ammiel in Lo Debar."

So King David had him brought from Lo Debar, from the house of Makir son of Ammiel.

When Mephibosheth son of Jonathan, the son of Saul, came to David, he bowed down to pay him honor.

David said, "Mephibosheth!"

"Your servant," he replied.

"Don't be afraid," David said to him, "for I will surely show you kindness for the sake of your father Jonathan. I will restore to you all the land that belonged to your grandfather Saul, and you will always eat at my table."

Mephibosheth bowed down and said, "What is your servant, that you should notice a dead dog like me?"

Then the king summoned Ziba, Saul's servant, and said to him, "I have given your master's grandson everything that belonged to Saul and his family. You and your sons and your servants are to farm the land for him and bring in the crops, so that your master's grandson may be provided for. And Mephibosheth, grandson of your master, will always eat at my table."

. . . So Mephibosheth ate at David's table like one of the king's sons.

Discuss

    1. How did Mephibosheth become crippled?
    2. Why did David want to find Mephibosheth?
    3. How did David keep his promise to Jonathan?
    4. Why is it important to keep our promises?

Pray

Dear Lord, help us to show love to others by being kind and by keeping our promises. Thank you for your faithfulness. Amen.

Sing—*The King of Love My Shepherd Is* (p. 201)

The King of love my shepherd is,
Whose goodness faileth never;
I nothing lack if I am his
And he is mine forever.

Do

Hang a heart on the Valentine tree each time you keep a promise.

Jesus often told stories that taught a lesson. This story teaches us about God's wonderful love for us.

Read—*Luke 15:11–24*

Jesus continued: "There was a man who had two sons. The younger one said to his father, 'Father, give me my share of the estate.' So he divided his property between them.

"Not long after that, the younger son got together all he had, set off for a distant country and there squandered his wealth in wild living. After he had spent everything, there was a severe famine in that whole country, and he began to be in need. So he went and hired himself out to a citizen of that country, who sent him to his fields to feed pigs. He longed to fill his stomach with the pods that the pigs were eating, but no one gave him anything.

"When he came to his senses, he said, 'How many of my father's hired men have food to spare, and here I am starving to death! I will set out and go back to my father and say to him: Father, I have sinned against heaven and against you. I am no longer worthy to be called your son; make me like one of your hired men.' So he got up and went to his father.

"But while he was still a long way off, his father saw him and was filled with compassion for him; he ran to his son, threw his arms around him and kissed him.

"The son said to him, 'Father, I have sinned against heaven and against you. I am no longer worthy to be called your son.'

"But the father said to his servants, 'Quick! Bring the best robe and put it on him. Put a ring on his finger and sandals on his feet. Bring the fattened calf and kill it. Let's have a feast and celebrate. For this son of mine was dead and is alive again; he was lost and is found.' So they began to celebrate."

Discuss

1. Why did the younger son want his father's money?
2. How do you think this made his father feel?
3. How did the father act toward his son—before he left, while he was gone, and when he returned?
4. What does this story teach us about God's love for us?

Final Thought

Jesus told this story because he wanted us to know how happy God is when we are sorry for our sin. It doesn't matter what bad things we have done or how many times we've done them. God loves us, forgives us, and welcomes us home.

Pray

Dear Father, thank you that you love us no matter what we do, and you never stop loving us. Help us to show that same kind of love to others. In Jesus' name. Amen.

Sing—*Just as I Am, without One Plea* (p. 202)

Just as I am, without one plea,
But that thy blood was shed for me,
And that thou bidd'st me come to thee,
O Lamb of God, I come, I come.

Just as I am, thou wilt receive,
Wilt welcome, pardon, cleanse, relieve;
Because thy promise I believe,
O Lamb of God, I come, I come.

Do

Hang a heart on your Valentine tree each time you do something loving for someone who has hurt you.

THE WEEK OF VALENTINE'S DAY

Here is another story Jesus told that contains an important lesson. Try to figure out what the lesson is as you listen.

Read—*Luke 10:25–37*

On one occasion an expert in the law stood up to test Jesus. "Teacher," he asked, "what must I do to inherit eternal life?"

"What is written in the Law?" he replied. "How do you read it?"

He answered: "'Love the Lord your God with all your heart and with all your soul and with all your strength and with all your mind'; and, 'Love your neighbor as yourself.'"

"You have answered correctly," Jesus replied. "Do this and you will live."

But he wanted to justify himself, so he asked Jesus, "And who is my neighbor?"

In reply Jesus said: "A man was going down from Jerusalem to Jericho, when he fell into the hands of robbers. They stripped him of his clothes, beat him and went away, leaving him half dead. A priest happened to be going down the same road, and when he saw the man, he passed by on the other side. So too, a Levite, when he came to the place and saw him, passed by on the other side. But a Samaritan, as he traveled, came where the man was; and when he saw him, he took pity on him. He went to him and bandaged his wounds, pouring on oil and wine. Then he put the man on his own donkey, took him to an inn and took care of him. The next day he took out two silver coins and gave them to the innkeeper. 'Look after him,' he said, 'and when I return, I will reimburse you for any extra expense you may have.'

"Which of these three do you think was a neighbor to the man who fell into the hands of robbers?"

The expert in the law replied, "The one who had mercy on him."

Jesus told him, "Go and do likewise."

Discuss

1. What happened to the man who was traveling?
2. Priests and Levites studied the Bible and knew all about God. Do you think this priest and Levite really loved God?
3. Samaritans were different, and Jews thought that they were no good. Do you think this was true?
4. What point was Jesus making with this story?

Final Thought

Mark Twain once said that it wasn't what he didn't understand about the Bible that bothered him. It was the part he did understand.

The "expert in the law" who questioned Jesus knew all the right answers. But Jesus told this story to illustrate that loving God is not a matter of knowing all the answers. We love him by doing what he says and by showing his love to others.

Pray

Father, help us to notice the people around us who need your love. Make us willing to show them your love and kindness. In Jesus' name. Amen.

Sing—*Take My Life, that I May Be* (pp. 188–89)

Take my hands and let them move
At the impulse of thy love;
Take my feet and let them be
Swift and beautiful for thee.

Do

Hang a heart on the Valentine tree each time you show kindness to someone who needs some love.

MOTHER'S DAY
AND
FATHER'S DAY

THE COMMANDMENT
WITH A PROMISE

We live in an age of unprecedented violence, particularly within the home. Almost any news day brings us stories of domestic violence: husbands beating wives and killing ex-wives, wives mutilating husbands, parents killing their own children, and children killing their parents. To say that the trend is alarming is to grossly understate the obvious.

But why is this happening? Social scientists, politicians, preachers, and theologians all have their theories. No doubt there are many factors involved.

I believe that the root cause is spiritual, and for whatever reasons, our culture has lost the concept of *honor,* or respect. The put-down humor of television sitcoms has permeated the homes of North America until parents expect sassing and sarcasm from their children (and in fact, employ these behaviors themselves). Just as Francis Schaeffer and C. Everett Koop predicted in the '70s, abortion and euthanasia have led to a loss of respect for life itself. Despite the proliferation of lawsuits for discrimination, harassment, and abuse, we see little respect in the workplace, in the media, or in the home.

Is respect so important? Absolutely! From Genesis to Revelation, the Bible consistently underscores the fundamental importance of respect—respect for God, respect for parents, respect for civil authorities, and respect for the individual (who is created in the image of God). The breakdown in respect propels a civilization toward chaos and anarchy.

The solution lies not in public policy or media reforms, although changes are desperately needed in these arenas. Rather, our culture will turn around as hearts begin to change, one by one by one. And parents still hold the position of greatest influence in the lives of their children, the next generation.

This is especially true with the issue of respect. Children who are trained to respect their parents much more readily learn to respect God, the civil law and authorities, teachers, employers, and peers. Interestingly enough, these are the children who are more likely to succeed in relationships and careers. Why? Because everyone likes to be treated with respect.

In fact, as the apostle Paul pointed out in Ephesians 6:2, the commandment to "honor your father and mother" is the first commandment with a promise: "that you may live long and that it may go well with you in the land the LORD your God is giving you" (Deut. 5:16).

Mother's Day and Father's Day are two days out of the year when our country pays tribute to parents. On these two holidays, we buy cards and gifts, make long-distance phone calls, serve breakfast in bed—all to say, "You are my parent, and you are worthy of honor."

Yes, we should honor our parents on Mother's Day and Father's Day. But let's not stop there. As Christians, we must set an example by honoring our parents and teaching our children to honor us. And we need to work at it daily.

Set a Good Example

Obviously, we will never train our children in respect if we ourselves do not treat others with respect. Although we can easily agree on this in principle, living it out is not always so simple. We all have blind spots when it comes to treating others respectfully.

I often fail at this when I am behind the wheel. The light turns yellow and I slow to a halt, but the driver behind me swerves into the next lane and blasts past me through the red light. "The light was red, you bozo!" I mutter. Fortunately, my daughter holds me accountable. "Mom, I hate it when you complain about other drivers! Can't you just keep your feelings to yourself?" She's right, of course. What kind of example am I when I call people names under my breath?

When it comes to showing respect, there is room for growth in all of us. Make this a goal for your entire family. *As you share your struggles and victories in this area, your children will be inspired to follow your example.* They will see how important respect is for you, and that is the first step toward making it a priority in their lives.

Root Out the Bad

Growing in respect also involves changing habits and deeply ingrained behavior patterns. It means rooting out bad habits and establishing new "holy habits" in their place.

My friend Sandy home-schools her children, Matt and Rebecca. She recalls her shock when Matt first sassed back at her. Where was this coming from? He didn't go to public school, so she couldn't blame it on ill-mannered peers. There were no children in the neighborhood from whom he could pick up those bad behaviors. The only children Matt spent time with were children from other strong Christian families. Finally it dawned on Sandy that it was simply in his nature, even as it was in her own. It's called "original sin." Disrespect comes naturally to all of us. It takes discipline and training to produce respectful behavior.

Clamping down on disrespectful speech is a good place to begin. From the time a child is old enough to speak, sassing and other forms of disrespectful speech must be met with swift and sure consequences.

Often parents let these behaviors slide until it is too late. Once a child is a teenager, options for discipline are limited, responsiveness to discipline is minimal, and patterns are indelibly marked in his or her personality.

Children are much more teachable in their early years. I urge you strongly to set high standards during this formative period. Children want to know what is expected of them. Young children must get the message that disrespect will not be tolerated. Never, ever abuse your children, but use firm, loving, consistent consequences to say, "We don't talk that way in our family."

Even older children need consistent consequences for speaking disrespectfully. My friend Steve related a recent incident in his home. His oldest son was heading to his room to do his homework and for some reason hurled a sarcastic remark at his mom. After counting to ten to get his emotions under control, Steve confronted his son.

"I'm sorry, but you're going to have to go to bed now," he informed him. "But, Dad! My homework!" his son protested. "You'll just have to face those consequences at school tomorrow," Steve said. Steve communicated that learning to treat family members with respect was more important for his son than completing that day's assignments.

What are some specific examples of disrespectful speech? Certainly anything that is demeaning, destructive, or hurtful. That would include put-down humor, sarcasm, name-calling, or yelling. Expressions like "shut-up" and "I hate you" do nothing to build loving relationships. And it doesn't take long for children to figure out just what to say to hurt their siblings' feelings or to push their parents' buttons. If it's hurtful, it should not be allowed.

Ephesians 4:29 gives us some good guidelines for acceptable and unacceptable speech. It says, "Do not let any unwholesome talk come out of your mouths, but only what is helpful for building others up according to their needs, that it may benefit those who listen." If we actually said only those things that fit these criteria, we would be much quieter! It would also have a profound effect on our family relationships. Our homes would be places of encouragement and mutual respect instead of war zones.

Hitting, biting, and other forms of physical violence are disrespectful. Any kind of abuse demeans the victim as well as the perpetrator. *We must guard against abuse in our homes*—parent against child, child against parent, child against child, and parent against parent. If one of the parents in the home demonstrates a pattern of abusive behavior, please seek immediate help from a trained professional. Children who grow up in abusive homes are likely to repeat the cycle when they grow up and have children.

Rather than abusing each other, we need to stand up for each other. It is very difficult to demand respect for oneself. How wonderful it is to have someone else stand up for you.

Build New Patterns of Respect

In addition to rooting out habits of disrespect, we must work at cultivating respectful behavior.

Jesus once told a story of an evil spirit who left a man and returned to the same man only to find that man's "house" (heart) unoccupied and swept clean. That spirit went out and found seven other spirits more wicked than itself. They all returned to the man and took up residence within him, placing him in a much worse condition than his original one (Matt. 12:43–45).

If we try to root out the bad patterns in our lives without replacing them with good patterns, we will find ourselves in the same situation as the man in Jesus' story. The bad patterns will return with a vengeance.

Here are some positive things we can do to show honor and build respect in our family relationships.

Manners show honor. The Japanese people value honor above all else. They also hold to rigorous standards in terms of manners. This is no coincidence. Manners and honor go hand in hand, for the use of good manners is one very tangible way in which we show honor to others.

No one is born with good manners. We must all be trained in them. Training children in good manners requires time, effort, and a certain amount of patience on the part of the parents. But the investment pays rich dividends.

Recently, Laura was invited to attend a concert at the Kennedy Center and to go out to dinner with the friend and her family. They dined in a nice Georgetown restaurant where waiters hovered and attended to their every need. Laura reported to me afterward that she had the best table manners of anyone at dinner. In fact, she was the only one to put her napkin in her lap. My response was, "Yea! Years of nagging pay off!"

Table manners are only one small part of manners in general. Telephone manners, introductions, greetings, thank-you notes—all these things and many more are important areas in which to teach our children good manners. Perhaps you need brushing up on these manners yourself! Check a book out of the library and read it as a family. With a lighthearted approach, learning manners can be fun.

Compliments show honor. The opposite of a put-down is a compliment. As long as they are sincere and are not empty flattery, compliments are a wonderful way to tell people that you respect, admire, and appreciate them.

One word of caution: Try to learn what kinds of compliments are meaningful to your family members. It took me a number of years to figure out that I was giving Jim the kind of compliments that I wanted to hear from him. But my compliments weren't doing a thing for him. He needed encouragement in completely different areas.

Several months ago I gave a family birthday celebration for my friend Karen. We went around the table and each said a prayer of thanks for something specific about her. Poor Karen was just about in tears by the end—and they weren't tears of happiness. Both of her boys had thanked God for her doing housework! "Is that what comes to mind when they think of me?" she asked me after dinner when we were alone.

If Karen's husband, Tim, had been there (he was out of town on business), I'm certain that he would have given the boys some direction. Children need to be clued in as to what compliments are appropriate and helpful and what things are better left unsaid.

Acts of thoughtfulness show honor. Often it is the little things that mean the most in expressing our respect for others. Nothing warms the heart like a simple note tucked in a lunch or on a pillow saying, "I love you. You mean so much to me."

Laura sometimes surprises me by setting the table or vacuuming and dusting the family room without my having asked her. Believe me, this is a wonderful way to honor your mother!

On the other hand, when someone works hard to make something look beautiful and another person treats it poorly, that shows disrespect or dishonor. When your child brings home an art project he has labored over for weeks, don't throw it in the garbage. Display it for all to see. That is how you honor your child.

Likewise, when Mom or Dad works hard to keep the house functional and neat, the children need to learn that picking up after themselves is a part of honoring their parents. This may seem like a losing battle, but keep at it. Make sure they understand the principles behind the commands.

Speaking well of others shows respect. First and foremost, we as adult children must speak well of our own parents. When our children overhear us complaining about our parents, what does that teach them about honoring one's parents?

And what about others in authority? Do our children hear us deriding the president of the United States, the governor, or the local law enforcement officers? Do we criticize our pastor or our Sunday school teacher? The primary way we can instill in our children a respect for authority is for us to exemplify it.

Instead of criticizing, we need to be looking for good things to praise in others. This is a whole new approach to life that runs counter to our natural tendency to criticize and complain. Yet Christ teaches that those who love him will be fountains of blessing, not cursing.

Let us make it our prayer that each day we will honor others and that our speech will bring blessing. Mother's Day and Father's Day are wonderful opportunities to begin a new family lifestyle of honoring others. We can honor the mother or father of the family by putting on our best manners and by giving sincere compliments. We can bless them in our words and actions and perform deeds of thoughtfulness that show them we appreciate and respect them.

But let's not stop there. Let us develop new habits of honoring each member of our family as we daily replace criticism with blessing and thoughtlessness with thoughtfulness. Then perhaps our families can begin to make a difference in restoring respect in our society.

FAMILY DEVOTIONS FOR MOTHER'S DAY

MOTHER'S DAY

YEAR 1

Being a mom is a hard job! Here's the story of a mother who had to use all her inventive powers just to keep her son alive!

Read—*Exodus 1:22–2:10*

Then Pharaoh gave this order to all his people: "Every boy that is born you must throw into the Nile, but let every girl live."

Now a man of the house of Levi married a Levite woman, and she became pregnant and gave birth to a son. When she saw that he was a fine child, she hid him for three months. But when she could hide him no longer, she got a papyrus basket for him and coated it with tar and pitch. Then she placed the child in it and put it among the reeds along the bank of the Nile. His sister stood at a distance to see what would happen to him.

Then Pharaoh's daughter went down to the Nile to bathe, and her attendants were walking along the river bank. She saw the basket among the reeds and sent her slave girl to get it. She opened it and saw the baby. He was crying, and she felt sorry for him. "This is one of the Hebrew babies," she said.

Then his sister asked Pharaoh's daughter, "Shall I go and get one of the Hebrew women to nurse the baby for you?"

"Yes, go," she answered. And the girl went and got the baby's mother. Pharaoh's daughter said to her, "Take this baby and nurse him for me, and I will pay you." So the woman took the baby and nursed him. When the child grew older, she took him to Pharaoh's daughter and he became her son. She named him Moses, saying, "I drew him out of the water."

Discuss

1. What problems did Moses' mother face?
2. How did she solve those problems?
3. What can we deduce about her from these verses?

4. What problems has the mom in your family faced? How has she worked creatively to solve them?

Final Thought

One of the reasons we celebrate mothers is that we realize the importance of a mother's love for her child. Children all depend on their mothers for food, protection, caretaking, and love. Even when life goes smoothly, it's not easy being a mom. But many mothers throughout history have brought children into a world where death lurks around the next corner, as in Moses' case. Love compels mothers to do whatever they can to ensure the safekeeping of their children. The love of mother for child is one of the most unselfish loves in this world. It gives us a glimpse of the self-sacrificing love of God in Jesus Christ.

Pray

Dearest Lord, thank you for giving mothers a special ability to love and care for their families. Thank you especially for our mom today. Bless her throughout the coming year. Amen.

Sing—*For the Beauty of the Earth* (p. 189)

For the joy of human love,
Brother, sister, parent, child,
Friends on earth and friends above;
For all gentle thoughts and mild:
Christ, our Lord, to you we raise
This our sacrifice of praise.

Do

Have each family member share one or two things about Mom that he or she most appreciates.

YEAR 2

Perhaps the most famous mother in all the world is Mary, the mother of Jesus. Yet we know very little about her. The important years during which she raised Jesus are summarized in one verse, Luke 2:40: "And the child grew and became strong; he was filled with wisdom, and the grace of God was upon him." We do have some glimpses of her that give us clues about the woman God chose to be the mother of his one and only Son.

Read—*Luke 1:39–49*

At that time Mary got ready and hurried to a town in the hill country of Judea, where she entered Zechariah's home and greeted Elizabeth. When Elizabeth heard Mary's greeting, the baby leaped in her womb, and Elizabeth was filled with the Holy Spirit. In a loud voice she exclaimed: "Blessed are you among women, and blessed is the child you will bear! But why am I so favored, that the mother of my Lord should come to me? As soon as the sound of your greeting reached my ears, the baby in my womb leaped for joy. Blessed is she who has believed that what the Lord has said to her will be accomplished!"

And Mary said:

"My soul praises the Lord
    and my spirit rejoices in God my Savior,
for he has been mindful
    of the humble state of his servant.
From now on all generations will call me blessed,
    for the Mighty One has done great things for me—
    holy is his name."

Discuss

1. What do Elizabeth's words tell us about Mary?
2. What was Mary feeling?
3. What do Mary's words indicate about what kind of a person she was?
4. How would these qualities make her a good mother for Jesus?

Final Thought

Mary's song (the Magnificat) continues for six more verses. The entire hymn is based on about twenty Old Testament verses. Mary must have known these verses by heart. Suddenly they came alive for her as she realized that she had a part in their fulfillment. Mary loved God, knew his Word, and believed that God would keep his promises. Certainly Mary must have prayed with Jesus and taught him about his heavenly Father. Mothers play a very important role in nurturing their children's faith.

Pray

Dear Lord, thank you for Mary's example of faith. Thank you for mothers of faith who have made a difference in our world. Today we especially thank you for our mother, and how her faith has helped us all to grow. In Jesus' name. Amen.

Sing—*What Child Is This* (p. 197)

So bring him incense, gold, and myrrh;
Come, peasant, king, to own him.
The King of kings salvation brings;
Let loving hearts enthrone him.
Raise, raise the song on high,
The virgin sings her lullaby;
Joy, joy, for Christ is born,
The babe, the son of Mary!

Do

Share how your mother's faith has made a difference in your life.

FAMILY DEVOTIONS
FOR FATHER'S DAY

YEAR 1

Every parent's worst nightmare is to have a child die. Nothing could be more painful. In the verses that follow, we read the story of a father whose twelve-year-old daughter was dying. He came to Jesus in desperation, hoping against hope that the Healer could do something to save his precious daughter.

Read—*Luke 8:41–42, 49–56*

Then a man named Jairus, a ruler of the synagogue, came and fell at Jesus' feet, pleading with him to come to his house because his only daughter, a girl of about twelve, was dying.

As Jesus was on his way, the crowds almost crushed him. . . .

While Jesus was still speaking, someone came from the house of Jairus, the synagogue ruler. "Your daughter is dead," he said. "Don't bother the teacher any more."

Hearing this, Jesus said to Jairus, "Don't be afraid; just believe, and she will be healed."

When he arrived at the house of Jairus, he did not let anyone go in with him except Peter, John and James, and the child's father and mother. Meanwhile, all the people were wailing and mourning for her. "Stop wailing," Jesus said. "She is not dead but asleep."

They laughed at him, knowing that she was dead. But he took her by the hand and said, "My child, get up!" Her spirit returned, and at once she stood up. Then Jesus told them to give her something to eat. Her parents were astonished, but he ordered them not to tell anyone what had happened.

Discuss

1. Who was Jairus?
2. What do you suppose Jairus was feeling when he found Jesus?
3. What does this tell us about what kind of a father he was?
4. How did Jesus respond to Jairus and his problem?

Final Thought

Jairus was a leader in the community. As such, he was used to being in control. Here was a situation where he was totally helpless. The one thing he could do was go to Jesus, someone who could help. Jairus is a wonderful example to Christian fathers. The wisest move a father can make is to bring his problems to Jesus.

Pray

Dear heavenly Father, we thank you that you care about our earthly fathers and the burdens of responsibility that they bear. Thank you for our dad and how much he cares for us. Assure him of your presence and your help, now and always. Amen.

Sing—*For the Beauty of the Earth* (p. 189)

For the joy of human love,
Brother, sister, parent, child,
Friends on earth and friends above;
For all gentle thoughts and mild:
Christ, our Lord, to you we raise
This our sacrifice of praise.

Do

Have each family member share one or two things about Dad that he or she most appreciates.

YEAR 2

There is something about serious illness that makes us turn to God. In this story, we read of a father whose son was close to death. Fortunately, Jesus was visiting a town that was about two days' journey from his home. The father couldn't make his son well, but he could find Jesus and try to convince him to come and heal his son.

Read—John 4:46–53

Once more he visited Cana in Galilee, where he had turned the water into wine. And there was a certain royal official whose son lay sick at Capernaum. When this man heard that Jesus had arrived in Galilee from Judea, he went to him and begged him to come and heal his son, who was close to death.

"Unless you people see miraculous signs and wonders," Jesus told him, "you will never believe."

The royal official said, "Sir, come down before my child dies."

Jesus replied, "You may go. Your son will live."

The man took Jesus at his word and departed. While he was still on the way, his servants met him with the news that his boy was living. When he inquired as to the time when his son got better, they said to him, "The fever left him yesterday at the seventh hour."

Then the father realized that this was the exact time at which Jesus had said to him, "Your son will live." So he and all his household believed.

Discuss

1. What did the father ask Jesus to do?
2. How did Jesus respond?
3. Why did the father leave without Jesus and without knowing that his son was healed?
4. What does this tell you about the father?

Final Thought

This father was both a man of action and a man of faith. When action was needed, he acted. He went to find Jesus when he knew that was his son's only hope. Yet when Jesus told him to go home because his son was healed, he exercised faith by obeying Jesus. He simply had to "take Jesus at his word." As a result, his entire household believed. Our world needs fathers who take Jesus at his word.

Pray

Heavenly Father, thank you for fathers who believe in you and lead their households in faith. Thank you especially for our dad and for his leadership. Help us to honor him. In Jesus' name. Amen.

Sing—*For the Beauty of the Earth* (p. 189)

For the joy of human love,
Brother, sister, parent, child,
Friends on earth and friends above;
For all gentle thoughts and mild:
Christ, our Lord, to you we raise
This our sacrifice of praise.

Do

Have each family member share one special memory of a time when Dad's faith or leadership inspired or helped him or her.

FAMILY DEVOTIONS FOR LENT: THE ROAD TO CALVARY

We are making "The Road to Calvary" available again by popular demand. For a daily devotional guide for your family's use at Lent, see *Family Celebrations at Easter* by Ann Hibbard, which also includes family worship on Easter, directions for a Holy Treasure Hunt, and a complete guide for a Christian family celebration of Passover.

Perhaps you have wondered, as I did, how to make the message of Easter real to your children. Then one December, as our family gathered for our Advent devotions, I thought, "We need to do this at Easter time! Preparing our hearts to celebrate Jesus' death and resurrection is even more important than preparing to celebrate his birth. More than anything else, I want my kids to understand why Jesus died and rose again—and what it means for us." To that end, I have written this section.

Since the early days of the church, Lent has been a season of self-examination, sorrow for sin, and commitment to Christ. It is the six-and-a-half-week period preceding Easter. These brief devotions, which begin the week of Ash Wednesday (seven weeks before Easter), take your family inside the drama of Jesus' last days, his arrest, crucifixion, and resurrection. There is one devotion per week until Palm Sunday. During Holy Week, daily family devotions are provided.

The Road to Calvary banner is a visual aid and teaching tool that coordinates with each of the devotions. (Complete instructions for making the banner can be found in the resources section at the back of the book.) At first the banner looks like an empty green hill set against a black sky. Every time your family gathers during Lent and Holy Week to read from God's Word, a gray felt circle is added to pave the road up to the crest of the hill. Each "paving stone" bears a symbol corresponding to the Bible verses the family reads that day. On Good Friday, the cross is placed at the top of the hill. The tomb is added on Saturday. Sunday morning, Easter, the family wakes up to see the dark Calvary banner covered up with a gold banner proclaiming HE IS RISEN.

Carve out of your schedule just ten or fifteen minutes each evening after supper. As you read, discuss, and pray together, you will meet Christ as a family in a new way, and your Easter season will be rich with his presence.

If you have just opened this book and Easter is only a week away, don't worry. It's not too late to begin! Simply jump in and do the family devotions for Holy Week. Next year you will be able to enjoy the entire Lenten season. Each evening as your family meets Christ in the upper room, in Gethsemane, and at the cross, you will experience the Easter story as never before.

WEEK 1 OF LENT

(SEVEN WEEKS BEFORE EASTER)

For the next six weeks, we will be preparing to celebrate Jesus' death and resurrection. First, let's discover why Jesus had to come to earth and die. To do this we need to start at the very beginning with Adam and Eve.

Read—*Genesis 3:1–13*

Now the serpent was more crafty than any of the wild animals the LORD God had made. He said to the woman, "Did God really say, 'You must not eat from any tree in the garden'?"

The woman said to the serpent, "We may eat fruit from the trees in the garden, but God did say, 'You must not eat fruit from the tree that is in the middle of the garden, and you must not touch it, or you will die.'"

"You will not surely die," the serpent said to the woman. "For God knows that when you eat of it your eyes will be opened, and you will be like God, knowing good and evil."

When the woman saw that the fruit of the tree was good for food and pleasing to the eye, and also desirable for gaining wisdom, she took some and ate it. She also gave some to her husband, who was with her, and he ate it. Then the eyes of both of them were opened, and they realized they were naked; so they sewed fig leaves together and made coverings for themselves.

Then the man and his wife heard the sound of the LORD God as he was walking in the garden in the cool of the day, and they hid from the LORD God among the trees of the garden. But the LORD God called to the man, "Where are you?"

He answered, "I heard you in the garden, and I was afraid because I was naked; so I hid."

And he said, "Who told you that you were naked? Have you eaten from the tree that I commanded you not to eat from?"

The man said, "The woman you put here with me—she gave me some fruit from the tree, and I ate it."

Then the LORD God said to the woman, "What is this you have done?"

The woman said, "The serpent deceived me, and I ate."

Discuss

1. What choice did the man and woman make?
2. How did they change after they disobeyed God?
3. Have an older child or adult read verses 14–24 and retell the story in his or her own words. What were the consequences of Adam and Eve's choice?
4. Do you think that if you tried hard, you could keep from doing anything wrong for the rest of your life? Why or why not?

Final Thought

Ever since Adam and Eve disobeyed God, people have wanted to do things their way instead of God's way. That is what sin is. This has brought many problems. Can you think of some? God promised a solution in verse 15. He said the woman's offspring would crush the serpent's head. When Jesus died and rose again, he crushed Satan's power forever.

Pray

Dear Lord, every day I disobey you. Thank you for sending me a savior, just as you promised. Amen.

Sing—*Just as I Am, without One Plea* (p. 202)

Just as I am, and waiting not
To rid my soul of one dark blot,
To thee, whose blood can cleanse each spot,
O Lamb of God, I come, I come.

Do

Place the symbol of the tree on the Road to Calvary banner. (Start at the bottom and work upward toward the crest of the hill.)

WEEK 2 OF LENT
(SIX WEEKS BEFORE EASTER)

This week we read about an event that pointed to Jesus' death.

Read—*Genesis 22:1–14*

Some time later God tested Abraham. He said to him, "Abraham!"

"Here I am," he replied.

Then God said, "Take your son, your only son, Isaac, whom you love, and go to the region of Moriah. Sacrifice him there as a burnt offering on one of the mountains I will tell you about."

Early the next morning Abraham got up and saddled his donkey. He took with him two of his servants and his son Isaac. When he had cut enough wood for the burnt offering, he set out for the place God had told him about. On the third day Abraham looked up and saw the place in the distance. He said to his servants, "Stay here with the donkey while I and the boy go over there. We will worship and then we will come back to you."

Abraham took the wood for the burnt offering and placed it on his son Isaac, and he himself carried the fire and the knife. As the two of them went on together, Isaac spoke up and said to his father Abraham, "Father?"

"Yes, my son?" Abraham replied.

"The fire and wood are here," Isaac said, "but where is the lamb for the burnt offering?"

Abraham answered, "God himself will provide the lamb for the burnt offering, my son." And the two of them went on together.

When they reached the place God had told him about, Abraham built an altar there and arranged the wood on it. He bound his son Isaac and laid him on the altar, on top of the wood. Then he reached out his hand and took the knife to slay his son. But the angel of the LORD called out to him from heaven, "Abraham! Abraham!"

"Here I am," he replied.

"Do not lay a hand on the boy," he said. "Do not do anything to him. Now I know that you fear God, because you have not withheld from me your son, your only son."

Abraham looked up and there in a thicket he saw a ram caught by its horns. He went over and took the ram and sacrificed it as a burnt offering instead of his son. So Abraham called that place The LORD Will Provide. And to this day it is said, "On the mountain of the LORD it will be provided."

Discuss

1. What did God tell Abraham to do? Why?
2. How do you think Abraham felt about this? What did he do?
3. What did Isaac ask his father? What did Abraham reply? Was Abraham right in his answer?
4. How does this point to Jesus' sacrifice?

Final Thought

God wanted to see if Abraham would obey him even if it meant sacrificing his promised son. God also wanted to point to a time when he, the Father, would sacrifice his one and only son, Jesus Christ, to take away our sin. In Jesus, God provided the lamb who died in our place.

Pray

Dear Lord, thank you that you provided yourself as the sacrifice for my sin. Amen.

Sing—*I Lay My Sins on Jesus* (p. 198)

I lay my sins on Jesus,
The spotless Lamb of God;
He bears them all and frees us
From the accursed load.
I bring my guilt to Jesus
To wash my crimson stains
Clean in his blood most precious
Till not a spot remains.

Do

Place the symbol of the altar on the Road to Calvary banner.

Do you remember the story of Moses and the burning bush? God told Moses to talk to Pharaoh. God wanted Pharaoh to let his people go so that they could move to the land that God had promised them. But Pharaoh didn't want to obey God. God gave Pharaoh many chances, but still Pharaoh wouldn't listen to him. Finally God had to cause a great disaster so that Pharaoh would listen. He had a special plan for the Israelites so that they would be safe from the disaster.

Read—*Exodus 12:21–30*

Then Moses summoned all the elders of Israel and said to them, "Go at once and select the animals for your families and slaughter the Passover lamb. Take a bunch of hyssop, dip it into the blood in the basin and put some of the blood on the top and on both sides of the doorframe. Not one of you shall go out the door of his house until morning. When the LORD goes through the land to strike down the Egyptians, he will see the blood on the top and sides of the doorframe and will pass over that doorway, and he will not permit the destroyer to enter your houses and strike you down.

"Obey these instructions as a lasting ordinance for you and your descendants. When you enter the land that the LORD will give you as he promised, observe this ceremony. And when your children ask you, 'What does this ceremony mean to you?' then tell them, 'It is the Passover sacrifice to the LORD, who passed over the houses of the Israelites in Egypt and spared our homes when he struck down the Egyptians.'" Then the people bowed down and worshiped. The Israelites did just what the LORD commanded Moses and Aaron.

At midnight the LORD struck down all the firstborn in Egypt, from the firstborn of Pharaoh, who sat on the throne, to the firstborn of the prisoner, who was in the dungeon, and the firstborn of all the livestock as well. Pharaoh and all his officials and all the Egyptians got up during the night, and there was loud wailing in Egypt, for there was not a house without someone dead.

Discuss

1. Why do you think this was called Passover?
2. The lamb was supposed to be a young male "without defect," or perfect. How was that lamb like Jesus?
3. What saved the Israelites from death?
4. How did Jesus save us? What do we need to do?

Final Thought

God made the way for the Israelites to be saved. Yet each Israelite family was responsible for putting the blood on the doorposts of their home. In the same way, God provided Jesus, the perfect Lamb, as the sacrifice for us. His blood saves us from eternal death. Yet each one of us must personally trust Christ as our Savior. It is like putting Jesus' blood on the doorframe of our hearts.

Pray

Dear Lord Jesus, thank you that you are that perfect Lamb of God who takes away the sin of the world. Amen.

Sing—*I Lay My Sins on Jesus* (p. 198)

I lay my sins on Jesus,
The spotless Lamb of God;
He bears them all and frees us
From the accursed load.
I bring my guilt to Jesus
To wash my crimson stains
Clean in his blood most precious
Till not a spot remains.

Do

Place the symbol of the lamb on the Road to Calvary banner.

Children, I hope that you never complain about the food your mom or dad puts before you. And parents, I certainly hope that you don't feed your children only a limited selection of foods that they like—pizza, hot dogs, and hamburgers! From an early age, our children learned that they were required to eat the foods I prepared for the entire family. If they complained, they were excused from the table and forfeited their meal. No snacks to tide them over until the next meal either! Contrary to popular belief, no child has ever died from missing one meal. In fact, hunger is a very good teacher.

In this story, Moses is leading the Israelites through the wilderness to the good land that God had promised them. When they had no food, God provided manna, a special bread from heaven that appeared on the ground every morning. When they had no water, God provided water for them, several times out of a rock. God showed them over and over again that he would take care of them. But still they complained.

Read—*Numbers 21:4–9*

They traveled from Mount Hor along the route to the Red Sea, to go around Edom. But the people grew impatient on the way; they spoke against God and against Moses, and said, "Why have you brought us up out of Egypt to die in the desert? There is no bread! There is no water! And we detest this miserable food!"

Then the LORD sent venomous snakes among them; they bit the people and many Israelites died. The people came to Moses and said, "We sinned when we spoke against the LORD and against you. Pray that the LORD will take the snakes away from us." So Moses prayed for the people.

The LORD said to Moses, "Make a snake and put it up on a pole; anyone who is bitten can look at it and live." So Moses made a bronze snake and put it up on a pole. Then when anyone was bitten by a snake and looked at the bronze snake, he lived.

Discuss

1. Why were the people dying?
2. Without God's help, could they make themselves better?
3. What special way did God make for the people to be saved?
4. Read John 3:14–15. Why did Jesus compare himself to the bronze serpent?

Final Thought

This true story points to Jesus and what he would come to do many years later. We are like the Israelites. We can't save ourselves from our sin any more than they could save themselves from the poisonous snakes. God sent Jesus, who was lifted up on the cross. If we look at him, or trust in him as our savior, we will be saved.

Pray

Lord, thank you that you came to save us from our sins. We look to you, trusting in your work on the cross to save us. Amen.

Sing—*My Faith Looks Up to Thee* (p. 203)

My faith looks up to thee,
Thou Lamb of Calvary,
Savior divine!
Now hear me while I pray,
Take all my guilt away,
Oh, let me from this day
Be wholly thine!

Do

Place the symbol of the serpent on the Road to Calvary banner.

WEEK 5 OF LENT

(THREE WEEKS BEFORE EASTER)

Jesus taught people by telling stories, or parables. Jesus knew that the Jewish leaders were planning to kill him. He also knew that he would die. That was the reason he came. He told this story to show them that God had sent him and that he was God's Son.

Read—Matthew 21:33–46

"Listen to another parable: There was a landowner who planted a vineyard. He put a wall around it, dug a winepress in it and built a watchtower. Then he rented the vineyard to some farmers and went away on a journey. When the harvest time approached, he sent his servants to the tenants to collect his fruit.

"The tenants seized his servants; they beat one, killed another, and stoned a third. Then he sent other servants to them, more than the first time, and the tenants treated them the same way. Last of all, he sent his son to them. 'They will respect my son,' he said.

"But when the tenants saw the son, they said to each other, 'This is the heir. Come, let's kill him and take his inheritance.' So they took him and threw him out of the vineyard and killed him.

"Therefore, when the owner of the vineyard comes, what will he do to those tenants?"

"He will bring those wretches to a wretched end," they replied, "and he will rent the vineyard to other tenants, who will give him his share of the crop at harvest time."

Jesus said to them, "Have you never read in the Scriptures:

"'The stone the builders rejected
   has become the capstone;
the Lord has done this,
   and it is marvelous in our eyes'?

"Therefore I tell you that the kingdom of God will be taken away from you and given to a people who will produce its fruit. He who falls on this stone will be broken to pieces, but he on whom it falls will be crushed."

When the chief priests and the Pharisees heard Jesus' parables, they knew he was talking about them. They looked for a way to arrest him, but they were afraid of the crowd because the people held that he was a prophet.

Discuss

1. Who are the people in this story? What happened?
2. The owner of the vineyard is really God. The tenants are the Jewish leaders. Who are the servants that God sent?
3. Who is the Son?
4. How did the Jewish leaders feel when Jesus told this story? Were they sorry for their sin? How do you know?

Final Thought

Jesus knew exactly what the evil rulers were thinking and planning. He knew what kind of death awaited him. Perhaps he even tried to upset them on purpose with this story so that they would hurry with their plans. It must have hurt God that the rulers he put in charge of his people, the Jews, would become so wicked.

Pray

Dear Lord, thank you for coming on purpose to die so that we could have a way to God. Amen.

Sing—*When I Survey the Wondrous Cross* (p. 205)

When I survey the wondrous cross
On which the prince of glory died,
My richest gain I count but loss
And pour contempt on all my pride.

Do

Place the symbol of the grapes on the Road to Calvary banner.

WEEK 6 OF LENT
(TWO WEEKS BEFORE EASTER)

Do you remember the story of Jesus raising Lazarus from the dead? Lazarus and his two sisters, Martha and Mary, were some of Jesus' best friends. Jesus sometimes stayed at their home in Bethany, which was just outside of Jerusalem. When Jesus knew that it was the time for him to go to Jerusalem to be arrested and crucified, it was only natural that he stay in Bethany with his good friends. Of course, they didn't know what was going to happen to Jesus. Only Jesus knew that. The story we are about to read took place exactly one week and one day before Jesus died. How do you think he felt as he dined with these dear friends, knowing that soon he was to die?

Read—*John 12:1–11*

Six days before the Passover, Jesus arrived at Bethany, where Lazarus lived, whom Jesus had raised from the dead. Here a dinner was given in Jesus' honor. Martha served, while Lazarus was among those reclining at the table with him. Then Mary took about a pint of pure nard, an expensive perfume; she poured it on Jesus' feet and wiped his feet with her hair. And the house was filled with the fragrance of the perfume.

But one of his disciples, Judas Iscariot, who was later to betray him, objected, "Why wasn't this perfume sold and the money given to the poor? It was worth a year's wages." He did not say this because he cared about the poor but because he was a thief; as keeper of the money bag, he used to help himself to what was put into it.

"Leave her alone," Jesus replied. "It was intended that she should save this perfume for the day of my burial. You will always have the poor among you, but you will not always have me."

Meanwhile a large crowd of Jews found out that Jesus was there and came, not only because of him but also to see Lazarus, whom he had raised from the dead. So the chief priests made plans to kill

Lazarus as well, for on account of him many of the Jews were going over to Jesus and putting their faith in him.

Discuss

1. What unusual thing did Mary do?
2. Why do you think Mary did this?
3. Who got mad about it? Why?
4. What did Jesus say about Mary's gift to him?

Final Thought

Jesus knew that this perfume was like Mary's savings account—it was all that she had. It was worth a year's wages. What is an average year's wages in your area? Mary was saying to Jesus, "I love you so much, Jesus, that I want to give you everything, even my most precious possession." Because this was probably her savings, Mary was trusting Christ to take care of her future. Do you think that Jesus wants us to give anything to him? What?

Pray

Dear Lord Jesus, you gave everything you had for me. Now I give you everything I am and have. Take control of my life and help me to live for you. Amen.

Sing—*When I Survey the Wondrous Cross* (p. 205)

Were the whole realm of nature mine,
That were a tribute far too small;
Love so amazing, so divine,
Demands my soul, my life, my all!

Do

Place the symbol of the perfume on the Road to Calvary banner.

PALM SUNDAY

The Jewish people had been waiting for hundreds of years for the Messiah, the one God would send to save them. They thought he would come as a great king who would make their country important and rich again. The Bible told them that this king would come into Jerusalem riding on a donkey.

Read—*Matthew 21:1–11*

As they approached Jerusalem and came to Bethphage on the Mount of Olives, Jesus sent two disciples, saying to them, "Go to the village ahead of you, and at once you will find a donkey tied there, with her colt by her. Untie them and bring them to me. If anyone says anything to you, tell him that the Lord needs them, and he will send them right away."

This took place to fulfill what was spoken through the prophet:

"Say to the Daughter of Zion,
 'See, your king comes to you,
gentle and riding on a donkey,
 on a colt, the foal of a donkey.'"

The disciples went and did as Jesus had instructed them. They brought the donkey and the colt, placed their cloaks on them, and Jesus sat on them. A very large crowd spread their cloaks on the road, while others cut branches from the trees and spread them on the road. The crowds that went ahead of him and those that followed shouted,

"Hosanna to the Son of David!"

"Blessed is he who comes in the name of the Lord!"

"Hosanna in the highest!"

When Jesus entered Jerusalem, the whole city was stirred and asked, "Who is this?"

The crowd answered, "This is Jesus, the prophet from Nazareth in Galilee."

Discuss

1. Jesus knew these verses from Zechariah. Why do you think he decided to ride into Jerusalem on a colt?
2. Why were the people so excited when they saw Jesus?
3. How do you think Jesus felt as he rode along to the crowd's cheers and praises?
4. How would Jesus be different than the people expected?

Final Thought

Jesus was the Messiah, that special king sent by God to save his people, but he came not to make them rich and important, but to save them from sin. The people were looking for outward changes. Jesus came to change hearts and to give us riches that would last forever—eternal life. That is far better! Has the gentle king come into your heart? What changes has he brought?

Pray

Dear Lord Jesus Christ, we praise you as King and Savior. Help us to serve and obey you as our king. Amen.

Sing—*Crown Him with Many Crowns* (p. 199)

Crown him with many crowns,
The Lamb upon his throne;
Hark, how the heav'nly anthem drowns
All music but its own.
Awake, my soul, and sing
Of him who died for thee,
And hail him as thy matchless king
Through all eternity.

Do

Place the symbol of the palm branch on the Road to Calvary banner.

MONDAY OF HOLY WEEK

Today we will be reading about the Last Supper, the last meal Jesus shared with his disciples. The meal was also a celebration of the Passover. Does anyone remember what the Passover was about? (Read Exodus 12:1–30 or summarize.) This was probably the most important celebration in Jesus' life.

Read—*Matthew 26:17–30*

On the first day of the Feast of Unleavened Bread, the disciples came to Jesus and asked, "Where do you want us to make preparations for you to eat the Passover?"

He replied, "Go into the city to a certain man and tell him, 'The Teacher says: My appointed time is near. I am going to celebrate the Passover with my disciples at your house.'" So the disciples did as Jesus had directed them and prepared the Passover.

When evening came, Jesus was reclining at the table with the Twelve. And while they were eating, he said, "I tell you the truth, one of you will betray me."

They were very sad and began to say to him one after the other, "Surely not I, Lord?"

Jesus replied, "The one who has dipped his hand into the bowl with me will betray me. The Son of Man will go just as it is written about him. But woe to that man who betrays the Son of Man! It would be better for him if he had not been born."

Then Judas, the one who would betray him, said, "Surely not I, Rabbi?"

Jesus answered, "Yes, it is you."

While they were eating, Jesus took bread, gave thanks and broke it, and gave it to his disciples, saying, "Take and eat; this is my body."

Then he took the cup, gave thanks and offered it to them, saying, "Drink from it, all of you. This is my blood of the covenant, which is poured out for many for the forgiveness of sins. I tell you, I will not drink of this fruit of the vine from now on until that day when I drink it anew with you in my Father's kingdom."

When they had sung a hymn, they went out to the Mount of Olives.

Discuss

1. What did Jesus say that upset the disciples?
2. Why do you think he mentioned this?
3. Breaking the unleavened bread and drinking the wine are important parts of Passover. What new meaning did Jesus give to these things?
4. How do you think Jesus was feeling?

Final Thought

Jesus knew which one of his disciples had become his enemy. He also knew that soon he would be arrested and deserted by his friends. And he knew how very hard it would be to die on the cross for the sins of the whole world. He knew how disappointed and confused his disciples would be when he died. What a sad and difficult celebration this must have been for Jesus!

Pray

Thank you, Lord Jesus, that your body was broken and your blood was shed for us. Amen.

Sing—*I Lay My Sins on Jesus* (p. 198)

I lay my sins on Jesus,
The spotless Lamb of God;
He bears them all and frees us
From the accursed load.
I bring my guilt to Jesus
To wash my crimson stains
Clean in his blood most precious
Till not a spot remains.

Do

Place the bread and wine symbol on the Road to Calvary banner.

TUESDAY OF HOLY WEEK

After the Passover meal, Jesus and his disciples went to a garden called Gethsemane on the Mount of Olives just outside Jerusalem, where Jesus often went to pray. Jesus told them that they would all desert him—that very night. He promised them that he would rise and go ahead of them into Galilee. Peter and the others insisted they would never desert Jesus. Jesus told Peter that on that very night, Peter would three times deny knowing Jesus.

Read—*Matthew 26:36–46*

Then Jesus went with his disciples to a place called Gethsemane, and he said to them, "Sit here while I go over there and pray." He took Peter and the two sons of Zebedee along with him, and he began to be sorrowful and troubled. Then he said to them, "My soul is overwhelmed with sorrow to the point of death. Stay here and keep watch with me."

Going a little farther, he fell with his face to the ground and prayed, "My Father, if it is possible, may this cup be taken from me. Yet not as I will, but as you will."

Then he returned to his disciples and found them sleeping. "Could you men not keep watch with me for one hour?" he asked Peter. "Watch and pray so that you will not fall into temptation. The spirit is willing, but the body is weak."

He went away a second time and prayed, "My Father, if it is not possible for this cup to be taken away unless I drink it, may your will be done."

When he came back, he again found them sleeping, because their eyes were heavy. So he left them and went away once more and prayed the third time, saying the same thing.

Then he returned to the disciples and said to them, "Are you still sleeping and resting? Look, the hour is near, and the Son of Man is betrayed into the hands of sinners. Rise, let us go! Here comes my betrayer!"

Discuss

1. What did Jesus go to Gethsemane to do? Why?
2. What were the disciples doing while Jesus was praying?
3. How do you think that made Jesus feel?
4. Why is it important to pray when we are very worried or upset about something?

Final Thought

We will never know the depth of sorrow that Jesus felt in the garden. Chances are, however, that we will know sorrow in our lives. When sorrow and trouble come, we must follow Christ's example and bring it to God in prayer. Prayer is not trying to get what we want from God. Even Jesus received a "no" from his Father. Rather, prayer is offering ourselves to God and accepting from him what he in his wisdom gives us.

Pray

Lord, so often we're like the disciples—we fall asleep instead of praying. Or we are just too busy for you. Help us to pray when we are upset or worried, giving our problems to you. Amen.

Sing—*I Lay My Sins on Jesus* (p. 198)

I lay my wants on Jesus;
All fullness dwells in him;
He heals all my diseases;
My soul he does redeem.
I lay my griefs on Jesus,
My burdens and my cares;
He from them all releases;
He all my sorrows shares.

Do

Place the symbol of the hand on the Road to Calvary banner.

WEDNESDAY OF HOLY WEEK

As Jesus was talking to his disciples in the garden, suddenly his enemies arrived. They were led by Judas, Jesus' disciple who became his enemy. They came to arrest Jesus and take him away. Jesus did not fight back or resist. He gave himself over to them of his own free will. The disciples, however, became frightened and ran away just as Jesus said they would.

First they brought Jesus before the Sanhedrin, the high court of the Jews, which included the chief priests, the elders, and the teachers of the law, seventy-one men in all. There they questioned Jesus. People told lies about Jesus. When Jesus told the truth about himself, the high priest flew into a rage. The leaders spit on Jesus and struck him with their fists. They decided that Jesus deserved to die.

But where did the disciples go? Peter must have followed secretly, for we find him sitting outside in the courtyard.

Read—*Matthew 26:69–75*

Now Peter was sitting out in the courtyard, and a servant girl came to him. "You also were with Jesus of Galilee," she said.

But he denied it before them all. "I don't know what you're talking about," he said.

Then he went out to the gateway, where another girl saw him and said to the people there, "This fellow was with Jesus of Nazareth."

He denied it again, with an oath: "I don't know the man!"

After a little while, those standing there went up to Peter and said, "Surely you are one of them, for your accent gives you away."

Then he began to call down curses on himself and he swore to them, "I don't know the man!"

Immediately a rooster crowed. Then Peter remembered the word Jesus had spoken: "Before the rooster crows, you will disown me three times." And he went outside and wept bitterly.

Discuss

1. What do you think Peter was doing out in the courtyard?
2. Why did Peter say that he didn't know Jesus?
3. What happened when the rooster crowed?
4. How do you suppose Peter felt?

Final Thought

It is easy to blame Peter for not standing up for Jesus, but it was a difficult situation. This was the middle of the night. Evil things were happening—you could feel it in the air. Perhaps Peter thought that he could be of more use to Jesus if he didn't get caught. But in the end he realized that fear had gotten the better of him. He had done what he said he would never do—disown Jesus. Are there times when we are afraid to stand up for Jesus?

Pray

Lord Jesus, help me not to be afraid to tell other people that I know you. Amen.

Sing—*Beneath the Cross of Jesus* (p. 192)

I take, O cross, your shadow
For my abiding place;
I ask no other sunshine
than the sunshine of his face.
Content to let the world go by,
To know no gain nor loss,
My sinful self my only shame,
My glory all, the cross.

Do

Place the symbol of the rooster on the Road to Calvary banner.

MAUNDY THURSDAY

The Jews did not want to break the law by killing Jesus, so they brought him to Pilate.

Read—*Matthew 27:11–26*

Meanwhile Jesus stood before the governor, and the governor asked him, "Are you the king of the Jews?"

"Yes, it is as you say," Jesus replied.

When he was accused by the chief priests and the elders, he gave no answer. Then Pilate asked him, "Don't you hear the testimony they are bringing against you?" But Jesus made no reply, not even to a single charge—to the great amazement of the governor.

Now it was the governor's custom at the Feast to release a prisoner chosen by the crowd. At that time they had a notorious prisoner, called Barabbas. So when the crowd had gathered, Pilate asked them, "Which one do you want me to release to you: Barabbas, or Jesus who is called Christ?" For he knew it was out of envy that they had handed Jesus over to him.

While Pilate was sitting on the judge's seat, his wife sent him this message: "Don't have anything to do with that innocent man, for I have suffered a great deal today in a dream because of him."

But the chief priests and the elders persuaded the crowd to ask for Barabbas and to have Jesus executed.

"Which of the two do you want me to release to you?" asked the governor.

"Barabbas," they answered.

"What shall I do, then, with Jesus who is called Christ?" Pilate asked.

They all answered, "Crucify him!"

"Why? What crime has he committed?" asked Pilate.

But they shouted all the louder, "Crucify him!"

When Pilate saw that he was getting nowhere, but that instead an uproar was starting, he took water and washed his hands in front of the crowd. "I am innocent of this man's blood," he said. "It is your responsibility!"

All the people answered, "Let his blood be on us and on our children!"

Then he released Barabbas to them. But he had Jesus flogged, and handed him over to be crucified.

Discuss

1. How did the Jews get Pilate to order Jesus' death?
2. When the Jews lied about Jesus, what did Jesus say? Why?
3. Did Pilate believe that Jesus was guilty or innocent? Why then did he give the order for Jesus to be killed?
4. What did he do to show that he was not responsible? Did that make him innocent of killing Jesus?

Final Thought

No one wanted to take responsibility for Jesus' death. The Jewish leaders tried to make Pilate responsible for doing the deed that they planned. Pilate insisted that the crowd of Jews was responsible, even though he ordered the death of a man he knew to be innocent. The fact is, all of these people were responsible. We too are responsible, for Jesus came to die because of our sin.

Pray

Lord, I confess that I have sinned, and my sin sent you to the cross. Forgive me. Thank you for dying for me. Amen.

Sing—*Alas! And Did My Savior Bleed* (p. 188)

Was it for sins that I had done
He groaned upon the tree?
Amazing pity, grace unknown,
And love beyond degree!

Do

Place the crown of thorns symbol on the Road to Calvary banner.

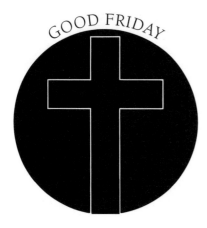

GOOD FRIDAY

Today we remember Jesus' death on the cross. Why is such a sad day called "Good Friday?"

Read—*Matthew 27:35–51*

When they had crucified him, they divided up his clothes by casting lots. And sitting down, they kept watch over him there. Above his head they placed the written charge against him: THIS IS JESUS, THE KING OF THE JEWS. Two robbers were crucified with him, one on his right and one on his left. Those who passed by hurled insults at him, shaking their heads and saying, "You who are going to destroy the temple and build it in three days, save yourself! Come down from the cross, if you are the Son of God!"

In the same way the chief priests, the teachers of the law and the elders mocked him. "He saved others," they said, "but he can't save himself! He's the King of Israel! Let him come down now from the cross and we will believe in him. He trusts in God. Let God rescue him now if he wants him, for he said, 'I am the Son of God.'" In the same way the robbers who were crucified with him also heaped insults on him.

From the sixth hour until the ninth hour darkness came over all the land. About the ninth hour Jesus cried out in a loud voice, *"Eloi, Eloi, lama sabachthani?"* which means, "My God, my God, why have you forsaken me?"

When some of those standing there heard this, they said, "He's calling Elijah."

Immediately one of them ran and got a sponge. He filled it with wine vinegar, put it on a stick, and offered it to Jesus to drink. The rest said, "Now leave him alone. Let's see if Elijah comes to save him."

And when Jesus had cried out again in a loud voice, he gave up his spirit.

At that moment the curtain of the temple was torn in two from top to bottom.

Discuss

1. What did people say about Jesus as he hung from the cross?
2. What did Jesus cry out? Why did he say this?
3. What did people think Jesus said?
4. What amazing thing happened the moment that Jesus died?

Final Thought

The greatest pain that Jesus felt was not the agony of hanging from a cross. It was the pain of being separated from God the Father. Jesus was carrying all our sin on him as he hung on the cross. Because God cannot even look on sin, he had to turn his face from Jesus. But here is the good news. When Jesus died, he made the way for us to know God. By tearing the curtain of the temple, God was showing us that he had opened the way for us to come to him.

Pray

Thank you, Lord Jesus, for dying for my sin so that I could come to God and know him, now and forever. Amen.

Sing—*Alas! And Did My Savior Bleed* (p. 188)

Alas! And did my Savior bleed,
And did my sov'reign die?
Would he devote that sacred head
For sinners such as I?

Was it for sins that I had done
He groaned upon the tree?
Amazing pity, grace unknown,
And love beyond degree!

Do

Place the cross at the top of the Road to Calvary banner.

SATURDAY

OF HOLY WEEK

Recently a six-year-old boy named Tory was playing in the baby pool area of a nearby pool. His mother did not see him run and jump into the main pool. Someone spotted him lying at the bottom of the pool. A twelve-year-old boy jumped in and pulled him out, but Tory was not breathing. His body was stiff and blue. One woman at the pool was a nurse. She immediately began cardiopulmonary resuscitation. The ambulance arrived and rushed Tory to the hospital. Miraculously, Tory lived. Even though he had gone for many minutes without oxygen, his brain was not damaged. If it had not been for the twelve-year-old who pulled him out and the nurse who did CPR, however, Tory would not be alive today. Today we read about someone who stepped in at a crisis. He did not save a life, but he took a big risk for Jesus.

Read—*Matthew 27:57–66*

As evening approached, there came a rich man from Arimathea, named Joseph, who had himself become a disciple of Jesus. Going to Pilate, he asked for Jesus' body, and Pilate ordered that it be given to him. Joseph took the body, wrapped it in a clean linen cloth, and placed it in his own new tomb that he had cut out of the rock. He rolled a big stone in front of the entrance to the tomb and went away. Mary Magdalene and the other Mary were sitting there opposite the tomb.

The next day, the one after Preparation Day, the chief priests and the Pharisees went to Pilate. "Sir," they said, "we remember that while he was still alive that deceiver said, 'After three days I will rise again.' So give the order for the tomb to be made secure until the third day. Otherwise, his disciples may come and steal the body and tell the people that he has been raised from the dead. This last deception will be worse than the first."

"Take a guard," Pilate answered. "Go, make the tomb as secure as you know how." So they went and made the tomb secure by putting a seal on the stone and posting the guard.

Discuss

1. What did Joseph ask of Pilate? Why do you suppose he did this?
2. What did he do with Jesus' body? Who saw him?
3. What did the Jewish leaders ask of Pilate?
4. Why were they worried?

Final Thought

It took courage for Joseph to go to Pilate and ask for Jesus' body, but his love for Jesus gave him courage. He honored Jesus by preparing his body and giving Jesus the expensive tomb he had bought for himself. The Jewish leaders went to Pilate out of fear. Their fear grew out of their hatred of Jesus. Interestingly, Pilate said yes to both requests. He was trying to stay neutral. Unfortunately for Pilate, there is no middle ground—we are either Jesus' friends or his enemies.

Pray

Dear Lord, help me to honor you as Joseph did, even when it may take a good deal of courage. Amen.

Sing—*Beneath the Cross of Jesus* (p. 192)

I take, O cross, your shadow For my abiding place;
I ask no other sunshine than The sunshine of his face;
Content to let the world go by, To know no gain nor loss,
My sinful self my only shame, My glory all, the cross.

Do

Place the symbol of the tomb on the right side of the Road to Calvary banner.

EASTER SUNDAY

Today is Easter, a celebration of the glorious day when Jesus was resurrected from the dead. The verses that we will read today are about a race.

Do you ever run races with your friends? Several years ago, Laura came home from school smiling proudly and boasting, "I can run faster than anyone in my class! When I run, none of the boys can catch me!" We were amused to hear that and wondered how many years it would be before Laura wanted the boys to catch her! Sometimes we run for the fun of running, and sometimes we run because we want to get someplace in a hurry. See if you can figure out why the people in these verses were running.

Read—*John 20:1–9*

Early on the first day of the week, while it was still dark, Mary Magdalene went to the tomb and saw that the stone had been removed from the entrance. So she came running to Simon Peter and the other disciple, the one Jesus loved, and said, "They have taken the Lord out of the tomb, and we don't know where they have put him!"

So Peter and the other disciple started for the tomb. Both were running, but the other disciple outran Peter and reached the tomb first. He bent over and looked in at the strips of linen lying there but did not go in. Then Simon Peter, who was behind him, arrived and went into the tomb. He saw the strips of linen lying there, as well as the burial cloth that had been around Jesus' head. The cloth was folded up by itself, separate from the linen. Finally the other disciple, who had reached the tomb first, also went inside. He saw and believed. (They still did not understand from Scripture that Jesus had to rise from the dead.)

Discuss

1. John, who is the writer, refers to himself here as "the other disciple." Why did he and Peter race to the tomb?

2. Who arrived first? Who entered the tomb first?
3. What did they see when they entered the tomb?
4. What do you think it means that John "saw and believed"?

Final Thought

Why do you suppose John included so many details in his account? I can think of two reasons. First, John was there himself and was writing exactly what he remembered. Sometimes when important things happen to us, it is the tiny details that stand out in our minds. Second, John wanted his readers to know that what he was writing was true, so that they would also believe that Jesus was risen from the dead. Giving a detailed account proved that John was there and had seen these things with his own eyes.

Pray

Dear Lord Jesus, thank you that you truly rose from the dead. Because you did, we know that you are the only Savior and Lord.

Sing—*Crown Him with Many Crowns* (p. 199)

Crown him with many crowns,
The Lamb upon his throne;
Hark, how the heav'nly anthem drowns
All music but its own.
Awake, my soul, and sing
Of him who died for thee,
And hail him as thy matchless king
Through all eternity.

Do

Flip the Road to Calvary banner over to show the Easter lilies and the words HE IS RISEN. (You may want to do this before the children awaken on Easter morning.)

INSTRUCTIONS:
BIRTHDAY FLAG
AND BIRTHDAY BANNER

W hat better way to honor a child on his or her birthday than to fly a special flag or hang a special banner that represents who he or she is?

Instructions are given for two options: an outdoor flag and an indoor banner. Those who sew will want to choose the outdoor flag, which involves machine stitching. Others may opt for the indoor banner, which requires a minimal amount of sewing.

If your home is not equipped with an outdoor flagpole, don't be dismayed. The materials list includes an inexpensive flagpole stand that is easily mounted on the outside of your house. You need not buy a flagpole; you can simply buy a dowel as specified in the materials list.

If you do have a flagpole in your yard, you will skip buying the flagpole stand and dowel. Instead, you will buy grommets to apply to your flag, so that you can hook it onto your flagpole.

The indoor banner is similar in concept to the outdoor flag, but it is made of materials that are not weatherproof. The component parts are glued, for the most part, rather than sewn.

Birthday Flag

Materials

- Two brown paper grocery bags
- Background fabrics: 3 feet by 5 feet brightly colored nylon or cotton (child's favorite color)
- Contrasting fabrics: 1 yard (for letters of child's name) or 1 yard of heavyweight iron-on interfacing (preferably nonwoven). See step 7 of instructions.
- Thread to match background fabrics
- Trim: 5 3/8 yards contrasting trim (optional)
- Flagpole: 1 rod, 3/4 inch diameter, 6 feet long
- Flagpole holder for 3/4-inch flagpole

Making the Flag

1. If you bought cotton fabric, preshrink the fabric by machine washing in hot water. Tumble dry and iron. Nylon need not be preshrunk.
2. Finish the edges of the background fabric. Fold raw edges in 1/4 inch. Fold again and machine stitch.
3. *Option 1.*
   Make casing for flagpole. Fold one of the 3-foot sides in 1 1/2 inches. Machine stitch 1/4 inch from inside edge. Stitch the top of the casing closed, as shown in Figure A.
   Option 2.
   If you already have a flagpole that uses hooks and grommets, install grommets in the corners of one of the 3-foot sides of the flag. (Follow the directions on the package for installing the grommets.)
4. If desired, sew contrasting trim to the front side of the flag around its perimeter and along the casing seam, as shown in Figure B.
5. Make patterns for the letters of the child's name out of the grocery bags. (For a five-letter name, the letters would be about 16 inches by 10 inches wide. Size will vary with the length of the child's name.)
6. Pin patterns to the contrasting fabric (or iron-on interfacing) and cut out letters.
7. *Option 1.*
   Appliqué the letters to the front side of the flag. (If your sewing machine does not do appliqué stitches, finish the raw edges of the letters and simply sew around the perimeter of the letters to attach them to the flag.)
   Option 2.
   If you are using iron-on interfacing instead of fabric, simply follow the directions that come with the interfacing for applying it to the flag background. The letters will be permanently affixed to the background without sewing.
8. Appliqué or iron on any other figures or symbols representing your child and his or her interests or achievements.

9. Slide flagpole into casing. The top end of the casing, which is sewn closed, will hold the flag on the end of the flagpole.
10. Attach flagpole holder to outside of house. Insert flagpole in flagpole holder.

To Use the Birthday Flag

Every year, appliqué one or more figures to the flag to represent interests, achievements, or special events from the previous year.

Fly the flag all day on the child's birthday. Also display the flag on other days that are special for your child. For instance, if your son wins the spelling bee at school, put his flag out to honor him.

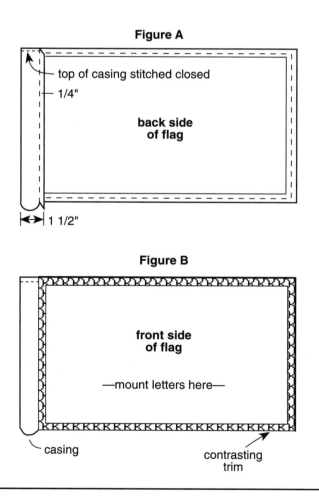

Figure A

top of casing stitched closed

1/4"

back side of flag

1 1/2"

Figure B

front side of flag

—mount letters here—

casing

contrasting trim

BIRTHDAY BANNER

Materials

- Felt background, 1/2 yard wide, length determined by number of letters in child's name. (For a five-letter name, 55 inches would be taken up by letters. A 60-inch length would be the minimum.)
- Felt sheets, 8 1/2 inches by 11 inches, one for each letter in the child's name, in a color that contrasts with the background color. Same number of sheets of paper, 8 1/2 inches by 11 inches.
- Appliqués or felt scraps to make figures to glue onto banner.
- Tacky glue (glue for fabrics)
- Thread to match background
- Decorative trim for banner (optional)
- 1 dowel, 5/8 inch diameter, 20 inches long
- 1 length of cord, 1/8 inch diameter, 36 inches long

Making the Birthday Banner

1. Fold top edge of banner over to the back side 1 1/2 inches. See Figure C.
2. Sew overlap 1 inch from fold and 1/2 inch from edge, as shown in Figure D. This forms the casing for the dowel.
3. Make patterns for the letters of your child's name on sheets of paper, 8 1/2 inches by 11 inches (one letter per sheet of paper, so that the letters are about 8 1/2 inches by 11 inches in size).
4. Cut out patterns and pin them to felt sheets. Cut out felt letters.
5. Glue felt letters to banner, as shown in Figure E.
6. Using felt scraps or other fabrics or materials, make figures representing interests or achievements of the child. Glue these to the banner.
7. Decorate the banner, if desired, with decorative trim. (For instance, glue or sew gold braid around perimeter of banner.)
8. Drill a hole in the dowel 3/4 inch from each end. See Figure F. If a drill is not available, use option 2 in step 10.

9. Insert dowel into casing.
10. *Option 1.*
    Stiffen ends of cord by wrapping with tape. Draw ends of cord through holes at ends of dowel and knot or tie cord. See Figure G.
    Option 2.
    Tie cord around ends of dowel. Glue cord to dowel so that cord will not slide toward center when hung. See Figure H.

To Use the Birthday Banner

Every year, glue one or more figures to the banner to represent interests, achievements, or special events from the previous year.

Hang the banner in a prominent place on the morning of the child's birthday. You may also want to hang the banner on other days that are special for your child.

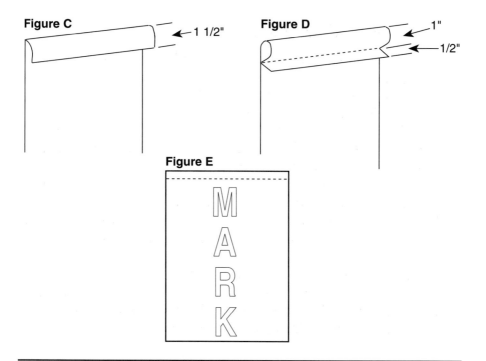

Figure C ← 1 1/2"

Figure D ← 1" ← 1/2"

Figure E

M
A
R
K

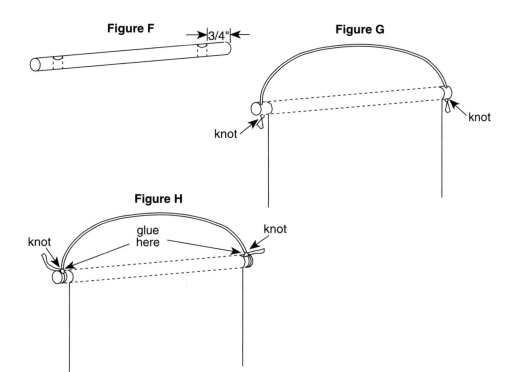

Figure F

3/4"

Figure G

knot

knot

Figure H

knot

glue
here

knot

knot

INSTRUCTIONS: VACATION SCRAPBOOK AND FEAST OF THE TABERNACLES

V acations can have their trying moments. Boredom is the frequent complaint of tired children, whether on a long car trip or at a cottage on a rainy day. To help alleviate this problem, two projects are offered here.

The first of these projects ties in with the family times—a vacation scrapbook. Some of the family times involve making things to add to the scrapbook. The second project builds on the theme of Moses and the Israelites in the wilderness, the subject of the family devotions for vacation.

Vacation Scrapbook

Materials

- Scrapbook
- Paper
- Crayons or markers
- Tape
- Scissors
- Camera and film
- Pencils
- Maps

Making the Scrapbook

This is an ongoing project, done bit by bit throughout the vacation. Before the vacation, you will need to purchase the scrapbook (or make one out of construction paper and paper fasteners) and assemble all the other materials. Pack all the project materials in one backpack, bag, or small box, and put it in a place that will be accessible during the trip.

Some of the family times will include an activity, such as drawing a picture or making a map, that can be put in the vacation scrapbook.

Fill the rest of the pages with mementos of your vacation. Photographs, travel brochures, and objects of nature all have a place in your vacation scrapbook.

Be sure to write down any funny incidents and include these accounts as well. This is a good activity for school-age children as they ride in the car. Have them write down events and incidents from the trip. Encourage them to use their senses—what did they smell, hear, feel, taste, and see?

You may want to keep a log of the activities of each day of your trip. This can provide the structure for the scrapbook. Day one would have the log of activities, as well as any photos or other mementos from that day's events.

Family vacations create memories for a lifetime—for you and your children. A vacation scrapbook can preserve these memories for years to come.

THE FEAST OF THE TABERNACLES

In the fall of every year, the Israelites remembered the years they wandered in the desert by celebrating the Feast of the Tabernacles, or the Feast of Booths. Families went out and made shelters out of branches and tree boughs. They lived in these "booths" for seven days, while they gathered in the fruit harvest. They did this so that they could understand what it was like for their forefathers to live in temporary shelters in the desert.

Can you imagine what it was like—all those Jewish families, with tiny children and old grandparents, together gathering sticks and boughs? They must have had lots of fun making their shelters.

You can try the same thing. But instead of making a full-sized shelter, make a model. Then while you are traveling on vacation, you can also remember the long journey of the Israelites.

Materials

- Twigs and small sticks
- Glue
- Straw or dried grass
- Paper

Making the Encampment

Decide where you will construct your model encampment. If you build it outdoors you will need a sheet of plastic to protect it from rain, and stones to anchor down the plastic. If you build it indoors (a good rainy-day activity, if you have a good spot to work), you will need a piece of cardboard, a box, or a sheet of poster board for a base for your encampment.

Break the twigs and sticks into appropriate lengths and construct little huts. You may want to make the walls individually, by gluing a row of sticks as they lie flat on the table. After the walls dry, they may be assembled (like a prefabricated house!). Make roofs out of sticks or straw glued on paper. Make your encampment as elaborate or as simple as you like.

INSTRUCTIONS:
VALENTINE TREE

Materials

- 1 tree branch (lightweight, but with lots of small branches)
- 1 pot or vase for holding tree branch
- Soil or rocks for weighting down pot or vase
- 1 piece of green poster board
- Pink, white, and red construction paper
- White yarn
- Scissors
- Glue or gluestick
- Paper punch
- An envelope, a plastic bag, or a basket for holding hearts
- Optional: paper doilies, glitter, crayons, markers

Making the Valentine Tree

1. Set tree branch (Valentine tree) in pot or vase. Support the branch by filling the vase or pot with soil or rocks.
2. Cut the pink, white, and red construction paper into 2-inch squares. Fold these in half and cut around edges so that they unfold in the shape of hearts. Make twenty to thirty per person.
3. Have each person decorate his or her own hearts. Use doilies, markers, glitter, or whatever you like.
4. Punch a hole in the top of each heart, about 1/4 inch from the top edge. String yarn through hole and make loop for hanging.
5. Keep the hearts near the tree in some form of container.

Using the Valentine Tree

Each of the four devotions during the Valentine season includes a special "action item." This is an action that each person should take in response to the Bible discussion. Usually it is an act of kindness. During the following week, each time someone does the specified act of kindness, that person may go to the Valentine tree and place a heart on one of the branches. By Valentine's Day, the tree should be full of hearts. More important, your family's hearts should be filled with the joy that comes from obeying God and showing his love to others.

INSTRUCTIONS: THE ROAD TO CALVARY BANNER

T he Road to Calvary banner is designed to enhance and re-
      inforce the family devotions for Lent as your family prepares
      to celebrate Christ's death and resurrection.
It is actually a double banner—the first banner depicts the road to
the cross, and the second proclaims the risen Christ. For each family
devotion a corresponding symbol is added on the road to the cross.
Then on Easter morning the cross banner is covered up by the gold
Easter banner. Jesus is risen! He has conquered sin and death!

Materials

- 1/2 yard of 36 inch-wide black felt
- 1/2 yard of 36-inch-wide green felt
- 1/2 yard of 36-inch-wide gold felt
- Green thread
- Gold thread
- Tacky glue (glue for fabrics)
- Fine tip black marker
- 13 adhesive-back Velcro fasteners—black circles *or* one 12-inch
  strip regular black Velcro (to be cut and sewn on)
- 1 dowel, 5/8 inch diameter, 21 inches long
- Felt sheets (8 1/2 inches by 11 inches) in the following colors
  and quantities: white (5), gray (2), purple (2), orange (1), red
  (1), brown (1), flesh (1), yellow (1)
- 1 length of cord, 1/8 inch diameter, 36 inches long

Making the Road to Calvary Banner

1. Cut the green felt in the shape of a hill, with the dimensions
   shown in Figure A. (Note: Save cut-away felt for later use.)
2. Sew hill to black background using green thread. Stitch around
   entire perimeter of green felt. See Figure B.
3. Trace and cut out the patterns on pages 181–85.
4. Cut out the felt pieces for each of the patterns cut in step 3.
   Colors and quantities are noted on the patterns.
5. Apply adhesive side of hook (fuzzy) Velcro fasteners to the center of the back of each gray felt circle. If you have regular
   Velcro, cut Velcro into 3/4-inch lengths. Hand sew hook

(fuzzy) Velcro fasteners to the center of the back of each gray felt circle. This is more time consuming than using the adhesive-back Velcro, but it is more durable.

6. Glue the felt figures onto the front side of the gray circles as shown on pages 181–85. (There will be thirteen circles.)

7. Apply adhesive side of loop Velcro fasteners to the green and black banner at the approximate locations shown in Figure C (thirteen total). If you are using regular Velcro, sew the loop fasteners at the appropriate locations.

8. Trace and cut out the patterns on pages 179–80. These patterns will be used to make the lilies and the words "HE IS RISEN."

9. Cut out the correct number of felt pieces for each of the patterns cut in step 8. (Note that the same lily and stamen patterns will be used for all three lilies and the smaller stem will be used for the lily on the left and on the right; simply reverse the pieces as shown in Figure D.)

10. Glue the felt pieces cut out in step 9 to the gold felt as shown in Figure D. Use a fine tip black marker to draw in the petals of the lilies and the overlapping lines of the leaves as shown on the patterns.

11. Sew gold banner to green and black banner along top edge using gold thread. See Figure E.

12. Sew a second seam 1 inch down from the first seam. See Figure E. This forms the casing for the dowel.

13. Drill a hole in the dowel 3/4 inch from each end. See Figure F. If a drill is not available, use option 2 in step 15.

14. Insert dowel into casing.

15. *Option 1.*
Stiffen ends of cord by wrapping with tape. Draw ends of cord through holes at ends of dowel and knot or tie cord. See Figure G.
Option 2.
Tie cord around ends of dowel. Glue cord to dowel so that cord will not slide toward center when hung. See Figure H.

Using the Road to Calvary Banner

1. Flip the Easter banner over, in back of the Calvary banner. Hang on wall.

2. Place gray felt circles in a manila envelope. Keep this envelope with your Bible and this book.

3. At the end of each devotional time allow a child to put the appropriate circle on the banner. Start from the bottom and work your way up to the cross, then over to the tomb. See the completed banner in Figure I.

4. On Easter Sunday, flip the Easter banner back over the road to Calvary.

Alternative

If you don't have the time or inclination to make the felt banner, use poster board and construction paper instead. Your children can color or paint the hill and cut out and glue the symbols. Then simply tape each circle to the poster as you go through your family times.

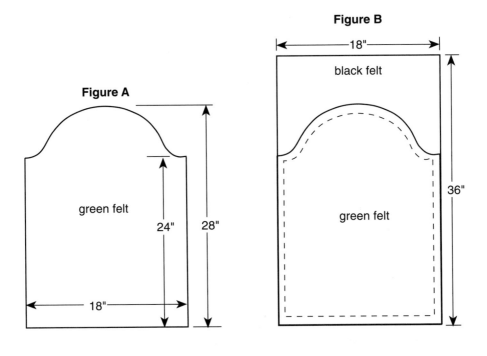

Figure C

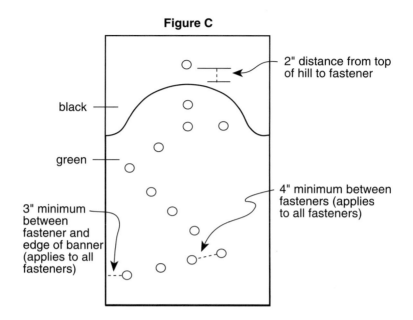

2" distance from top of hill to fastener

black

green

4" minimum between fasteners (applies to all fasteners)

3" minimum between fastener and edge of banner (applies to all fasteners)

Figure D

HE IS

RISEN

Figure E

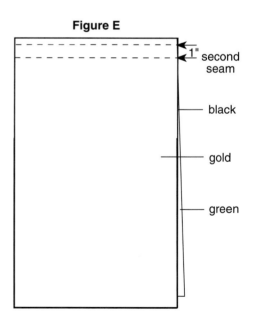

1" second seam

black

gold

green

Figure F

|← 3/4" →|

Figure G

knot

knot

Figure H

knot

glue here

knot

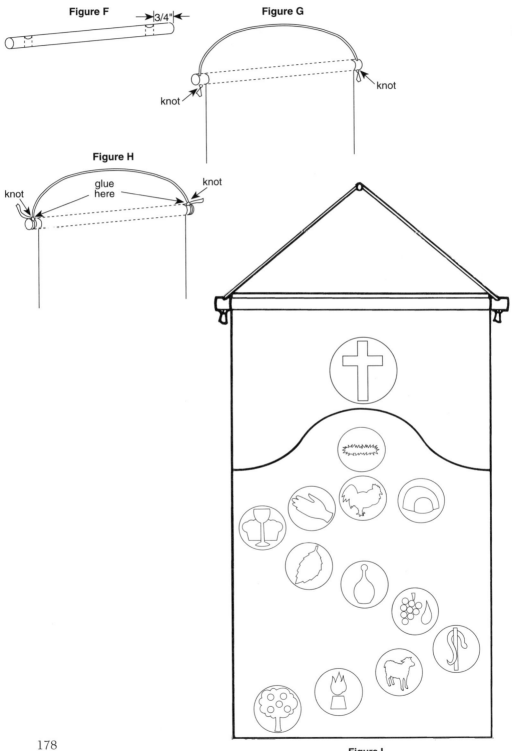

Figure I

Cut these letters out of purple felt.

Enlarge these letters to 150%
on a copy machine before tracing.

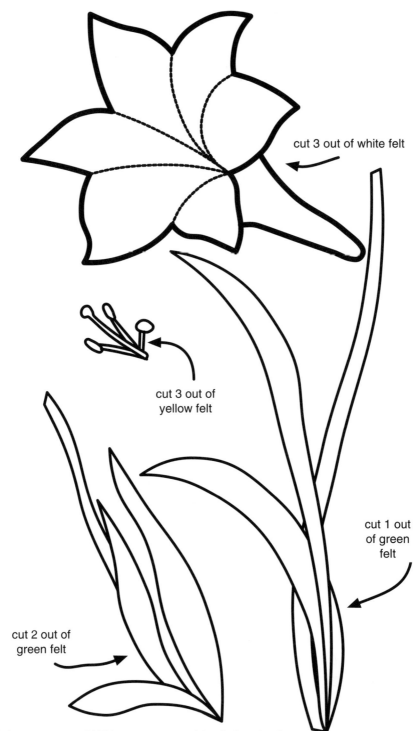

cut 3 out of white felt

cut 3 out of
yellow felt

cut 1 out
of green
felt

cut 2 out of
green felt

Enlarge patterns 142% on a copy machine before tracing.

red
(cut 5)

green

gray

orange

gray

brown

white

gray

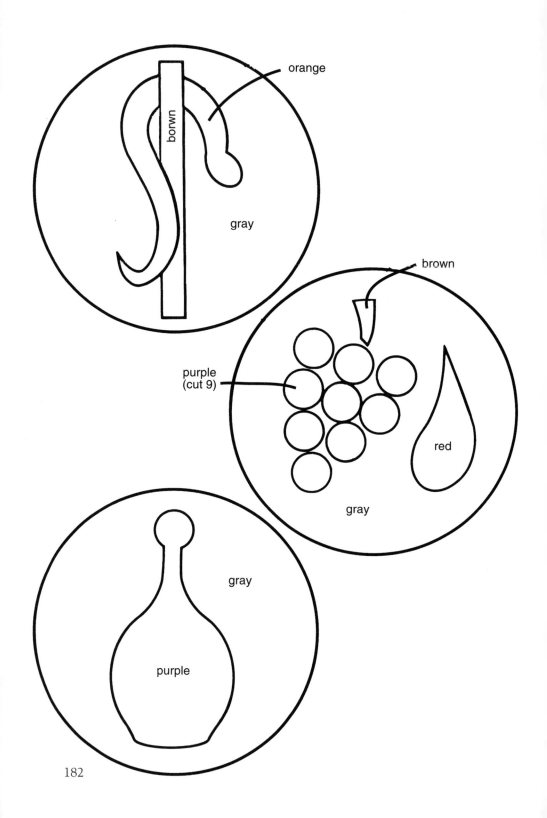

orange

borwn

gray

brown

purple
(cut 9)

red

gray

gray

purple

182

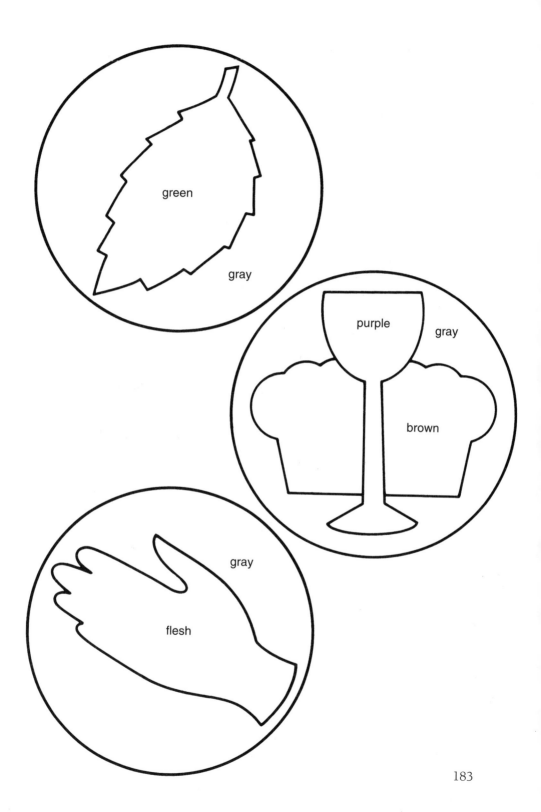

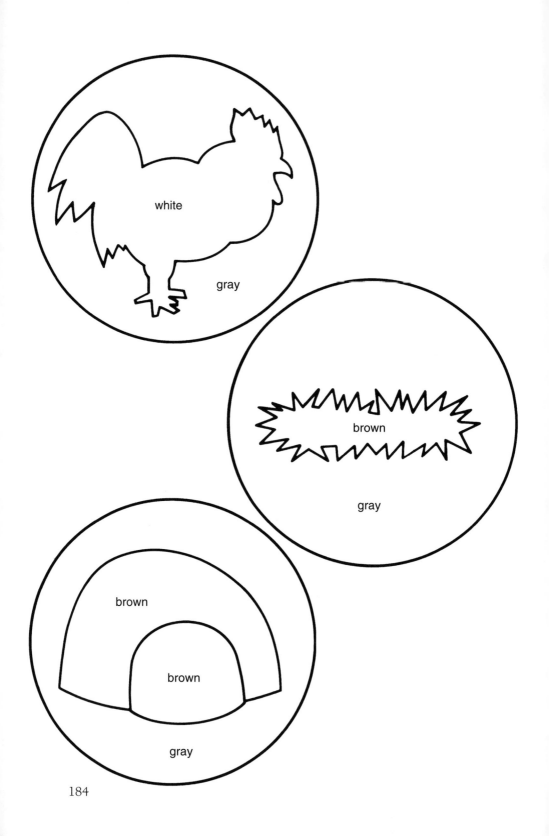

white

gray

brown

gray

brown

brown

gray

184

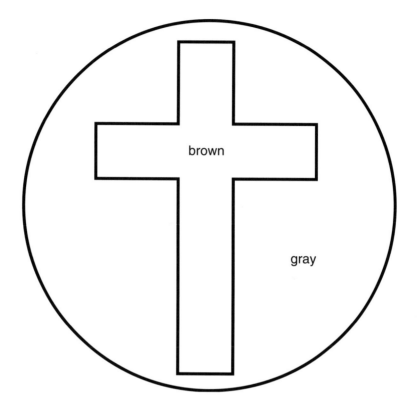

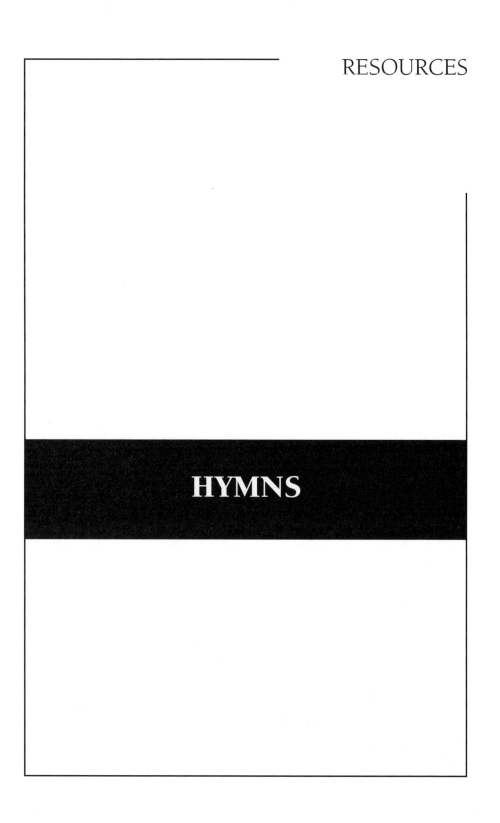

HYMNS

Alas! And Did My Savior Bleed

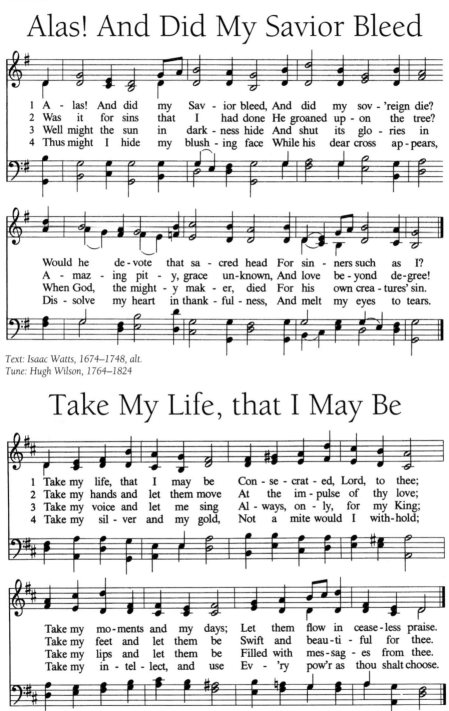

1 A - las! And did my Sav - ior bleed, And did my sov - 'reign die?
2 Was it for sins that I had done He groaned up - on the tree?
3 Well might the sun in dark - ness hide And shut its glo - ries in
4 Thus might I hide my blush - ing face While his dear cross ap - pears,

Would he de - vote that sa - cred head For sin - ners such as I?
A - maz - ing pit - y, grace un - known, And love be - yond de - gree!
When God, the might - y mak - er, died For his own crea - tures' sin.
Dis - solve my heart in thank - ful - ness, And melt my eyes to tears.

Text: Isaac Watts, 1674–1748, alt.
Tune: Hugh Wilson, 1764–1824

Take My Life, that I May Be

1 Take my life, that I may be Con - se - crat - ed, Lord, to thee;
2 Take my hands and let them move At the im - pulse of thy love;
3 Take my voice and let me sing Al - ways, on - ly, for my King;
4 Take my sil - ver and my gold, Not a mite would I with-hold;

Take my mo - ments and my days; Let them flow in cease - less praise.
Take my feet and let them be Swift and beau - ti - ful for thee.
Take my lips and let them be Filled with mes - sag - es from thee.
Take my in - tel - lect, and use Ev - 'ry pow'r as thou shalt choose.

5 Take my will and make it thine;
It shall be no longer mine.
Take my heart, it is thine own;
It shall be thy royal throne.

6 Take my love; my Lord, I pour
At thy feet its treasure store;
Take myself, and I will be
Ever, only, all for thee.

Text: Frances R. Havergal, 1836–1879, alt.
Tune: William H. Havergal, 1793–1870

For the Beauty of the Earth

1 For the beau-ty of the earth, For the beau-ty of the skies,
2 For the won-der of each hour Of the day and of the night,
3 For the joy of ear and eye, For the heart and mind's de-light,
4 For the joy of hu-man love, Broth-er, sis-ter, par-ent, child,

For the love which from our birth O-ver and a-round us lies:
Hill and vale and tree and flow'r, Sun and moon and stars of light:
For the mys-tic har-mo-ny Link-ing sense to sound and sight:
Friends on earth and friends a-bove; For all gen-tle thoughts and mild:

Refrain
Christ, our Lord, to you we raise This our sac-ri-fice of praise.

Text: Folliott S. Pierpoint, 1835–1917, alt.
Tune: Conrad Kocher, 1786–1872

Oh, Worship the King

1 Oh, wor - ship the King, all - glo - rious a - bove.
2 Oh, tell of his might; oh, sing of his grace,
3 The earth with its store of won - ders un - told,
4 Your boun - ti - ful care what tongue can re - cite?

Oh, grate - ful - ly sing his pow'r and his love;
Whose robe is the light, whose can - o - py space;
Al - might - y, your pow'r has found - ed of old;
It breathes in the air, it shines in the light,

Our shield and de - fend - er, the An - cient of Days,
His char - iots of wrath the deep thun - der - clouds form,
Es - tab - lished it fast by a change - less de - cree,
It streams from the hills, it de - scends to the plain,

Pa - vil - ioned in splen - dor, and gird - ed with praise.
And dark is his path on the wings of the storm.
And round it has cast, like a man - tle, the sea.
And sweet - ly dis - tills in the dew and the rain.

5   Frail children of dust, and feeble as frail,
       In you do we trust, nor find you to fail;
       Your mercies, how tender, how firm to the end,
       Our maker, defender, redeemer, and friend.

Text: Robert Grant, 1779–1838, alt.
Tune: William Croft, 1678–1727

Praise, My Soul, the King of Heaven

1 Praise, my soul, the King of heav - en; To his feet your trib - ute bring.
2 Praise him for his grace and fa - vor To our fore-bears in dis - tress.
3 Ten - der - ly he shields and spares us; Well our fee - ble frame he knows.
4 An - gels help us to a - dore him, Who be - hold him face to face.

Ran-somed, healed, re-stored, for - giv - en, Ev - er - more his prais - es sing.
Praise him, still the same for - ev - er, Slow to chide and swift to bless.
In his hands he gent - ly bears us, Res - cues us from all our foes.
Sun and moon bow down be - fore him; All who dwell in time and space.

Al - le - lu - ia! Al - le - lu - ia! Praise the ev - er - last - ing King!
Al - le - lu - ia! Al - le - lu - ia! Glo - rious in his faith - ful - ness!
Al - le - lu - ia! Al - le - lu - ia! Wide - ly as his mer - cy flows.
Al - le - lu - ia! Al - le - lu - ia! Praise with us the God of grace.

Text: Henry F. Lyte, 1793–1847, alt.
Tune: John Goss, 1800–1880

Beneath the Cross of Jesus

1 Be - neath the cross of Je - sus I long to take my stand;
2 Up - on the cross of Je - sus, My eye at times can see
3 I take, O cross, your shad - ow For my a - bid - ing place;

The shad - ow of a might - y rock With - in a wea - ry land,
The ver - y dy - ing form of one Who suf - fered there for me.
I ask no oth - er sun - shine than The sun - shine of his face;

A home with-in a wil - der - ness, A rest up - on the way,
And from my con - trite heart, with tears, Two won - ders I con - fess:
Con - tent to let the world go by, To know no gain nor loss,

From the burn - ing of the noon - tide heat And bur - dens of the day.
The won - der of his glo - rious love And my un - wor - thi - ness.
My sin - ful self my on - ly shame, My glo - ry all, the cross.

Text: Elizabeth C. Clephane, 1830–1869
©Tune: Frederick C. Maker, 1844–1927

Guide Me Ever, Great Redeemer

1 Guide me ev - er, great Re-deem - er, Pil - grim through this
2 O - pen now the crys - tal foun - tain Where the heal - ing
3 When I tread the verge of Jor - dan, Bid my anx - ious

bar - ren land. I am weak, but you are might - y; Hold me
wa - ters flow; Let the fire and cloud - y pil - lar Lead me
fears sub - side; Death of death and hell's de - struc - tion, Land me

with your pow'r - ful hand. Bread of heav - en, bread of heav - en,
all my jour - ney through. Strong de - liv - 'rer, strong de - liv - 'rer,
safe on Ca - naan's side. Songs and prais - es, songs and prais - es,

Feed me now and ev - er - more, Feed me now and ev - er - more.
Shield me with your might - y arm, Shield me with your might - y arm.
I will raise for - ev - er - more, I will raise for - ev - er - more.

Text: William Williams, 1717–1791; tr. composite, alt.
©Tune: John Hughes, 1873–1932

193

O Word of God Incarnate

1 O Word of God in - car - nate, O Wis - dom from on high,
2 The Church from you, dear Mas - ter, Re - ceived the gift di - vine;
3 Oh, make your Church, dear Sav - ior, A lamp of bur - nished gold

O Truth un-changed, un-chang - ing, O Light of our dark sky:
And still that light is lift - ed O'er all the earth to shine.
To bear be - fore the na - tions Your true light, as of old;

We praise you for the ra - diance That from the hal - lowed page,
It is the chart and com - pass That, all life's voy - age through,
Oh, teach your wan-d'ring pil - grims By this their path to trace,

A lan - tern to our foot - steps, Shines on from age to age.
Mid mists and rocks and quick - sands Still guides, O Christ, to you.
Till, clouds and dark - ness end - ed, They see you face to face.

Text: William W. How, 1823–1897, alt.
Tune: Neu-vermehrtes Gesangbuch, Meiningen, 1693

Immortal, Invisible, God Only Wise

1 Im - mor - tal, in - vis - i - ble, God on - ly wise, In
2 Un - rest - ing, un - hast - ing, and si - lent as light, Nor
3 To all, life thou giv - est, to both great and small; In
4 Thou reign - est in glo - ry; thou dwell - est in light; Thine

light in - ac - ces - si - ble hid from our eyes, Most
want - ing, nor wast - ing, thou rul - est in might; Thy
all life thou liv - est, the true life of all; We
an - gels a - dore thee, all veil - ing their sight; All

bless - ed, most glo - rious, the An - cient of Days, Al -
jus - tice like moun - tains high soar - ing a - bove Thy
blos - som and flour - ish like leaves on the tree, And
laud we would ren - der; oh, help us to see 'Tis

might - y, vic - to - rious, thy great name we praise!
clouds which are foun - tains of good - ness and love.
with - er and per - ish, but naught chang - eth thee.
on - ly the splen - dor of light hid - eth thee!

Text: W. Chalmers Smith, 1824–1908, alt.
Tune: Welsh folk tune

Joyful, Joyful We Adore Thee

1 Joy-ful, joy-ful we a-dore thee, God of glo-ry, Lord of love!
2 All thy works with joy sur-round thee, Earth and heav'n re-flect thy rays,
3 Thou art giv-ing and for-giv-ing, Ev-er bless-ing, ev-er blest,

Hearts un-fold like flow'rs be-fore thee, Prais-ing thee, their sun a-bove.
Stars and an-gels sing a-round thee, Cen-ter of un-bro-ken praise.
Well-spring of the joy of liv-ing, O-cean-depth of hap-py rest!

Melt the clouds of sin and sad-ness, Drive the gloom of doubt a-way.
Field and for-est, vale and moun-tain, Flow-'ry mead-ow, flash-ing sea,
Thou our Fa-ther, Christ our broth-er, All who live in love are thine;

Giv-er of im-mor-tal glad-ness, Fill us with the light of day.
Chant-ing bird, and flow-ing foun-tain Call us to re-joice in thee.
Teach us how to love each oth-er, Lift us to the joy di-vine!

©*Text: Henry van Dyke, 1852–1933*
Tune: Ludwig van Beethoven, 1770–1827, adapt.

What Child Is This

1 What child is this, who, laid to rest, On Mar-y's lap is sleep-ing?
2 Why lies he in such mean es-tate Where ox and ass are feed-ing?
3 So bring him in-cense, gold, and myrrh; Come, peas-ant, king, to own him.

Whom an-gels greet with an-thems sweet While shep-herds watch are keep-ing?
Good Chris-tian, fear; for sin-ners here The si-lent Word is plead-ing.
The King of kings sal-va-tion brings; Let lov-ing hearts en-throne him.

This, this is Christ the king, Whom shep-herds guard and an-gels sing;
Nails, spear shall pierce him through, The cross be borne for me, for you;
Raise, raise the song on high, The vir-gin sings her lul-la-by;

Haste, haste to bring him laud, The babe, the son of Mar - y!
Hail, hail the Word made flesh, The babe, the son of Mar - y!
Joy, joy, for Christ is born, The babe, the son of Mar - y!

Text: William C. Dix, 1837–1898
Tune: English ballad, 16th cent.

197

I Lay My Sins on Jesus

1 I lay my sins on Je - sus, The spot - less Lamb of God;
2 I lay my wants on Je - sus; All full - ness dwells in him;
3 I rest my soul on Je - sus, This wea - ry soul of mine;

He bears them all and frees us From the ac - curs - ed load.
He heals all my dis - eas - es; My soul he does re - deem.
His right hand me em - brac - es; I on his breast re - cline.

I bring my guilt to Je - sus To wash my crim - son stains
I lay my griefs on Je - sus, My bur - dens and my cares;
I love the name of Je - sus, Im - man - uel, Christ, the Lord;

Clean in his blood most pre - cious Till not a spot re - mains.
He from them all re - leas - es; He all my sor - rows shares.
Like fra - grance on the breez - es His name a - broad is poured.

Text: Horatius Bonar, 1808–1889
Tune: Neu-vermehrtes Gesangbuch, Meiningen, 1693

Crown Him with Many Crowns

1 Crown him with man-y crowns, The Lamb up-on his throne; Hark,
2 Crown him the vir-gin's Son, The God in-car-nate born, Whose
3 Crown him the Lord of love— Be-hold his hands and side, Rich
4 Crown him the Lord of life, Who tri-umphed o'er the grave And

how the heav'n-ly an-them drowns All mu-sic but its own. A-
arm those crim-son tro-phies won Which now his brow a-dorn; Fruit
wounds, yet vis-i-ble a-bove, In beau-ty glo-ri-fied. No
rose vic-to-rious in the strife For those he came to save. His

wake, my soul, and sing Of him who died for thee, And
of the mys-tic rose, Yet of that rose the stem, The
an-gels in the sky Can ful-ly bear that sight, But
glo-ries now we sing, Who died and rose on high, Who

hail him as thy match-less king Through all e-ter-ni-ty.
root whence mer-cy ev-er flows, The babe of Beth-le-hem.
down-ward bend their burn-ing eyes At mys-ter-ies so bright.
died, e-ter-nal life to bring, And lives that death may die.

Text: Matthew Bridges, 1800–1894; Godfrey Thring, 1823–1903
Tune: George J. Elvey, 1816–1893

What a Friend We Have in Jesus

1 What a friend we have in Je - sus, All our sins and griefs to bear!
2 Have we tri - als and temp - ta - tions? Is there trou - ble an - y - where?
3 Are we weak and heav - y - lad - en, Cum - bered with a load of care?

What a priv - i - lege to car - ry Ev - 'ry-thing to God in prayer!
We should nev - er be dis - cour-aged— Take it to the Lord in prayer.
Pre-cious Sav - ior, still our ref - uge— Take it to the Lord in prayer.

Oh, what peace we of - ten for - feit; Oh, what need-less pain we bear—
Can we find a friend so faith - ful Who will all our sor - rows share?
Do your friends de-spise, for - sake you? Take it to the Lord in prayer.

All be-cause we do not car - ry Ev - 'ry-thing to God in prayer!
Je - sus knows our ev - 'ry weak-ness— Take it to the Lord in prayer.
In his arms he'll take and shield you; You will find a so - lace there.

Text: Joseph Scriven, 1820–1886
Tune: Charles C. Converse, 1832–1918

The King of Love My Shepherd Is

1 The King of love my shep-herd is, Whose good - ness
2 Where streams of liv - ing wa - ter flow, My ran - somed
3 Per - verse and fool - ish oft I strayed, But yet in
4 In death's dark vale I fear no ill, With thee, dear

fail - eth nev - er; I noth - ing lack if
soul he lead - eth And, where the ver - dant
love he sought me, And on his shoul - der
Lord, be - side me, Thy rod and staff my

I am his And he is mine for - ev - er.
pas - tures grow, With food ce - les - tial feed - eth.
gent - ly laid, And home, re - joic - ing, brought me.
com - fort still; Thy cross be - fore to guide me.

5 Thou spreadst a table in my sight;
   Thine unction grace bestoweth;
  And, oh, what transport of delight
   From thy pure chalice floweth!

6 And so, through all the length of days,
   Thy goodness faileth never.
  Good Shepherd, may I sing thy praise
   Within thy house forever.

Text: Henry W. Baker, 1821–1877
Tune: Irish

Just as I Am, without One Plea

1 Just as I am, with-out one plea, But that thy blood was shed for me,
2 Just as I am, and wait-ing not To rid my soul of one dark blot,
3 Just as I am, though tossed a-bout With man-y a con-flict, man-y a doubt,
4 Just as I am, poor, wretch-ed, blind; Sight, rich-es, heal-ing of the mind,

And that thou bidd'st me come to thee,
To thee, whose blood can cleanse each spot,
Fight-ings and fears with-in, with-out,   O Lamb of God, I come, I come.
Yea, all I need, in thee to find,

5 Just as I am, thou wilt receive,
Wilt welcome, pardon, cleanse, relieve;
Because thy promise I believe,
O Lamb of God, I come, I come.

6 Just as I am; thy love unknown
Has broken ev'ry barrier down;
Now to be thine, yea, thine alone,
O Lamb of God, I come, I come.

Text: Ray Palmer, 1808–1887
Tune: Lowell Mason, 1792–1872

My Faith Looks Up to Thee

1 My faith looks up to thee, Thou Lamb of Cal - va - ry,
2 May thy rich grace im - part Strength to my faint - ing heart,
3 While life's dark maze I tread And griefs a - round me spread,
4 When ends life's tran - sient dream, When death's cold, sul - len stream

Sav - ior di - vine! Now hear me while I pray, Take all my
My zeal in - spire; As thou hast died for me, Oh, may my
Be thou my guide; Bid dark - ness turn to day, Wipe sor - row's
Shall o'er me roll; Blest Sav - ior, then, in love Fear and dis -

guilt a - way, Oh, let me from this day Be whol - ly thine!
love to thee Pure, warm, and change - less be, A liv - ing fire!
tears a - way, Nor let me ev - er stray From thee a - side.
trust re - move; Oh, bear me safe a - bove, A ran - somed soul!

Text: Ray Palmer, 1808–1887
Tune: Lowell Mason, 1792–1872

All People That on Earth Do Dwell

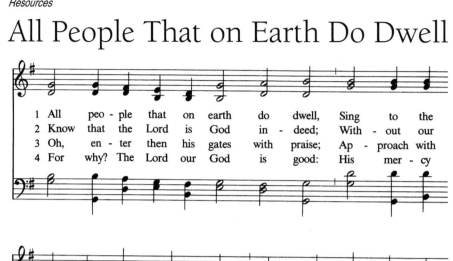

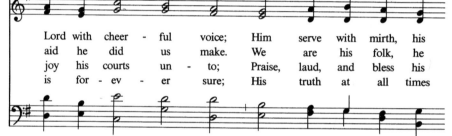

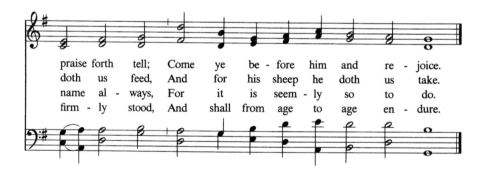

5 To Father, Son, and Holy Ghost,
   The God whom heav'n and earth adore,
   From us and from the angel host
   Be praise and glory evermore.

Text: William Kethe, d. c. 1593
Tune: Louis Bourgeois, c. 1510–1561

When I Survey the Wondrous Cross

1 When I sur - vey the won - drous cross On which the
2 For - bid it, Lord, that I should boast Save in the
3 See, from his head, his hands, his feet, Sor - row and
4 Were the whole realm of na - ture mine, That were a

prince of glo - ry died, My rich - est gain I
death of Christ, my God; All the vain things that
love flow min - gled down. Did e'er such love and
trib - ute far too small; Love so a - maz - ing,

count but loss And pour con - tempt on all my pride.
charm me most, I sac - ri - fice them to his blood.
sor - row meet, Or thorns com - pose so rich a crown?
so di - vine, De - mands my soul, my life, my all!

Text: Isaac Watts, 1674–1748
Tune: adapt. Edward Miller, 1731–1807

Savior, like a Shepherd Lead Us

1 Sav - ior, like a shep-herd lead us; Much we need your ten - der care.
2 We are yours; in love be-friend us, Be the guard - ian of our way;
3 You have prom-ised to re - ceive us, Poor and sin - ful though we be;
4 Ear - ly let us seek your fa - vor, Ear - ly let us do your will;

In your pleas-ant pas - tures feed us, For our use your fold pre - pare.
Keep your flock,from sin de - fend us, Seek us when we go a - stray.
You have mer - cy to re - lieve us, Grace to cleanse, and pow'r to free.
Bless-ed Lord and on - ly Sav - ior, With your love our spir - its fill.

Bless-ed Je - sus, bless - ed Je - sus, You have bought us; we are yours.
Bless-ed Je - sus, bless - ed Je - sus, Hear us chil - dren when we pray.
Bless-ed Je - sus, bless - ed Je - sus, Ear - ly let us turn to you.
Bless-ed Je - sus, bless - ed Je - sus, You have loved us, love us still.

Text: Dorothy A. Thrupp, 1779–1847
Tune: Ludvig M. Lindeman, 1812–1887

Before You, Lord, We Bow

1 Be - fore you, Lord, we bow, Our God who reigns a - bove And
2 The na - tion you have blest May well your love de - clare, From
3 May ev - 'ry moun - tain height, Each vale and for - est green, Shine
4 Earth, hear your Mak - er's voice; Your great Re - deem - er own; Be -

rules the world be - low, Bound-less in pow'r and love. Our thanks we
foes and fears at rest, Pro - tect - ed by your care. For this bright
in your Word's pure light, And its rich fruits be seen! May ev - 'ry
lieve, o - bey, re - joice, And wor - ship him a - lone. Cast down your

bring in joy and praise, Our hearts we raise to you, our king!
day, for this fair land— Gifts of your hand— our thanks we pay.
tongue be tuned to praise And join to raise a grate - ful song.
pride, your sin de - plore, And bow be - fore the Cru - ci - fied.

5   And when in pow'r he comes,
     Oh, may our native land
     From all its rending tombs
     Send forth a glorious band,
     A countless throng, with joy to sing
     To heav'n's high king salvation's song!

Text: Francis S. Key, 1779–1843, alt.
Tune: John Darwall, 1731–1789

Index of Hymns